Garden Of Verses

Volume 1

ELLA RITA UQUAK

Write and Release
PUBLISHING

www.writeandreleasepublishing.com

ACKNOWLEDGEMENT

To Him, who started it all, and saw me through every winding path, to the finishing line, I give Him all the glory. In the enchanting notes of the bloomy,"Garden Of Verses" and the flourishing rhythms of joy, God is exalted.

Walking through the tunes of time, they lit my path with lingering fragrance of love, and bountiful notes of joy, showering me with rides of affection, my parents, Prof Isaac Solomon Dema, and Joan Dema, of blessed memories. Thanks for all the love.

To my wonder man, delightful, and energetic, passionate, and success driven, my love, my hubby, who supported, and encouraged me tremendously, and has been greatly excited to see this venture come to fruition, as it makes its way to the pages of reality, my Special Thanks....

To my treasured, adorable, cherished, and loving children, Charles Jr, and Joshua, who showed admiration for the work, while in process, and gave words of encouragement, which boosted me, I appreciate your love, and support.

In their own special, and beautiful way, my loving brothers who have greatly touched my life, with many interesting, memorable moments, and expressed joy, on getting this book out. Denis gave words of encouragement, and expressed delight on the project, Akenobi, greatly encouraged and inspired me to get the work out, Perisuo showed sweet sentiments, as he voiced out congratulations, on the project. My brothers, my joy, and to Idiami for all the fun times, we shared while, he walked the isles of mortality.

Sweetly, and preciously, with such vibrance and warmth, they have added zest to my life, my lovely, adorable, sisters-in-law Bernice, Lizzy, Pat, and Sarah, I appreciate you all.

To a very special lady, who has walked many miles with me, stood by me, and showered me with unwavering love, Mrs Iminabo Opuoyibo, my friend, my sister, you are amazing.

Table of Contents

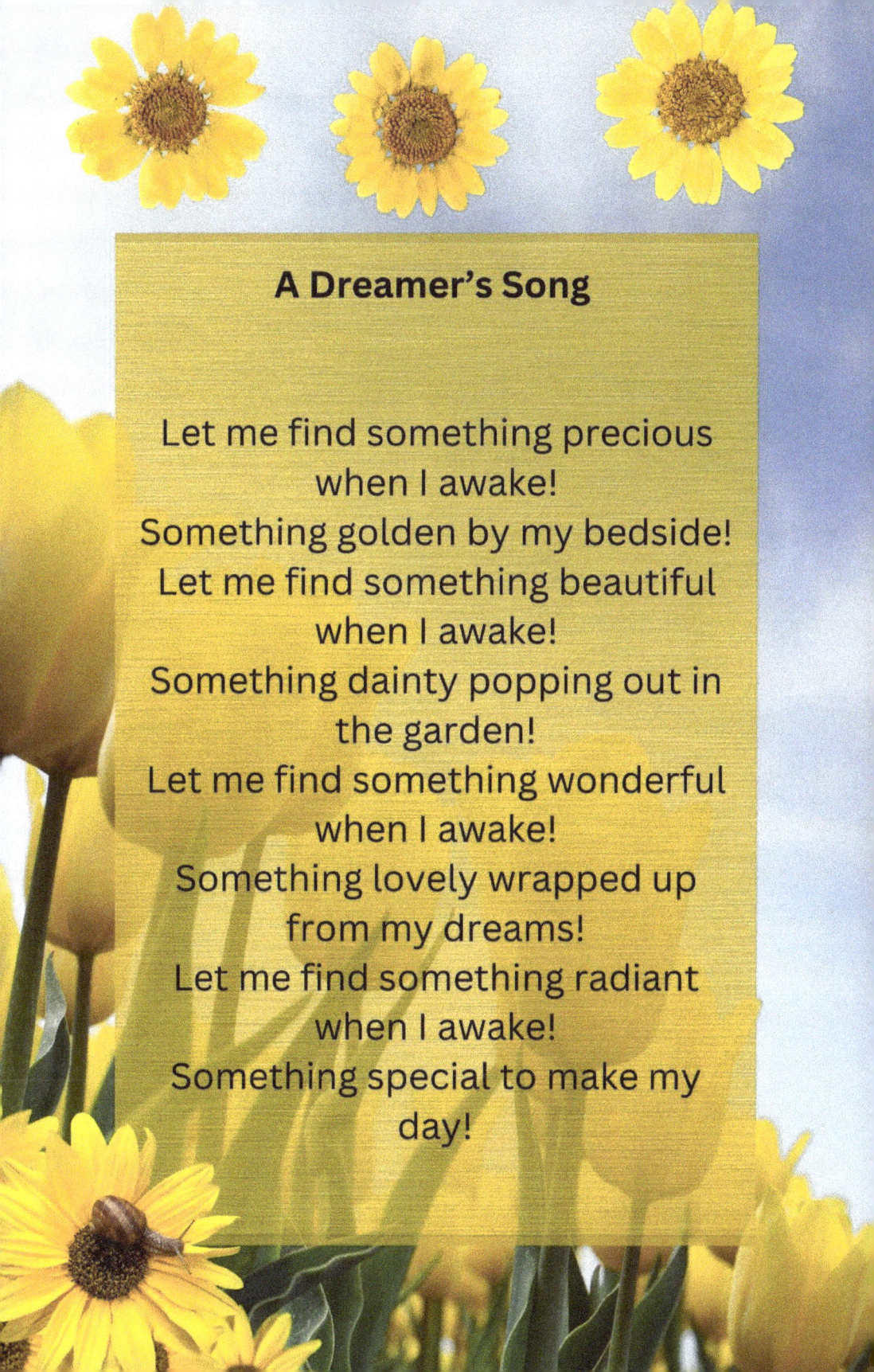

A Dreamer's Song

Let me find something precious
when I awake!
Something golden by my bedside!
Let me find something beautiful
when I awake!
Something dainty popping out in
the garden!
Let me find something wonderful
when I awake!
Something lovely wrapped up
from my dreams!
Let me find something radiant
when I awake!
Something special to make my
day!

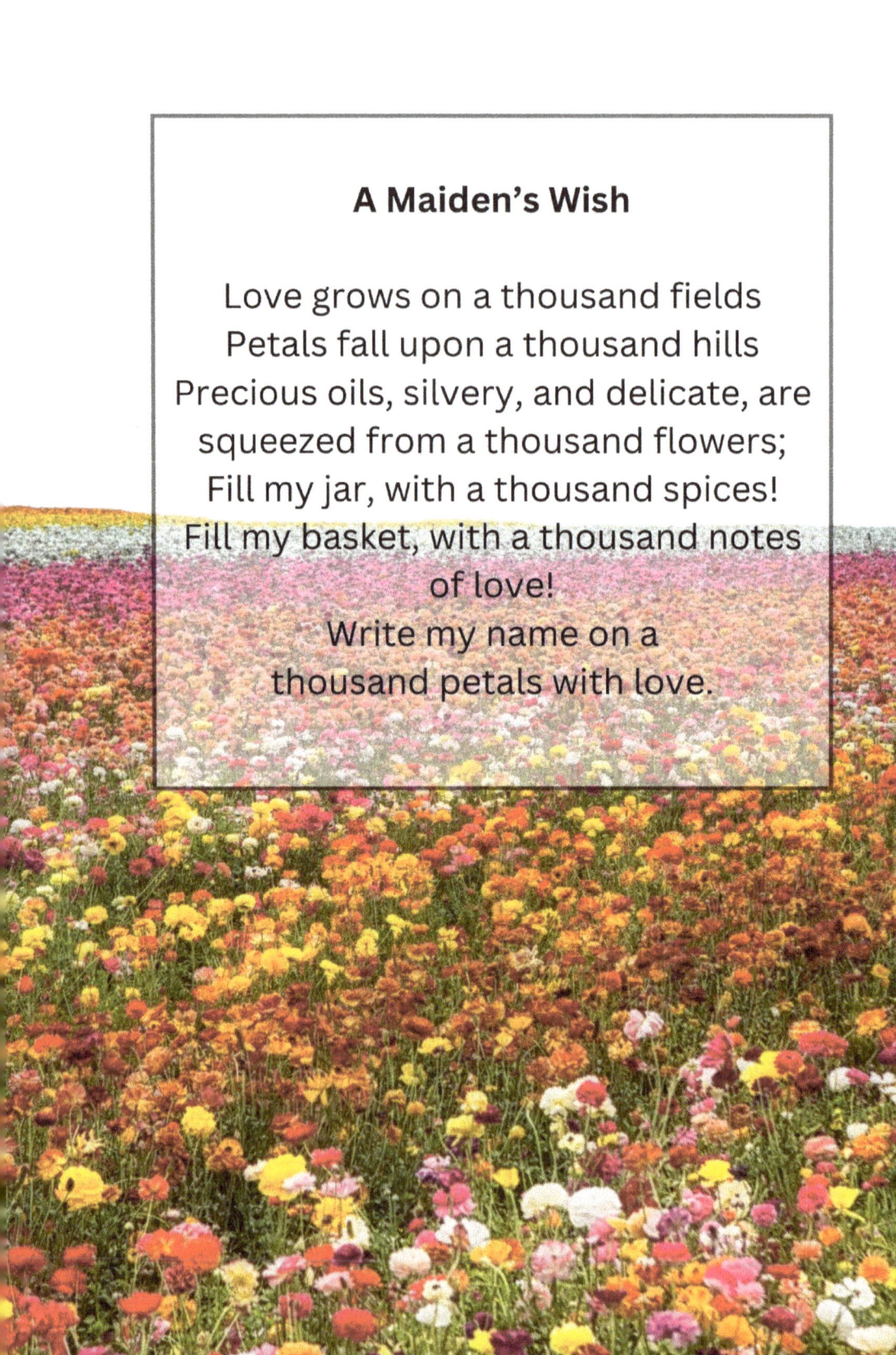

A Maiden's Wish

Love grows on a thousand fields
Petals fall upon a thousand hills
Precious oils, silvery, and delicate, are
squeezed from a thousand flowers;
Fill my jar, with a thousand spices!
Fill my basket, with a thousand notes
of love!
Write my name on a
thousand petals with love.

A New Dawn

Sweet scent of
daffodils!
The reawakening
of beauty;
Echoes of joy!
Sparkling notes
of Spring!
It's a game of florals,
It's a rebirth of
a new season!
It's a new dawn!

A Rose Delight

She is a Rose delight!
A sweet damsel of the
Summer sun!
Radiant and Blushing!
Pearly and Delectable!
It's a Rose delight to
be frilly-n-flamboyant!

A Rose

It's its sweetness, that makes a rose,
so precious!
It's the joy it exudes, that makes a
rose, so lovable!
It's its elegance, and flamboyance,
that makes a rose, so adorable!
A rose, for its glamour, is special!
A-Rose-For-A-Rose, is beautiful.

Always With Us

God is always with us!
In our "Highs" and in
our "Lows"
In our "Darkest" hour,
In our "Brightest"
moment;
He is always with us.

Aura Of Delight

There's an aura of delight where,
the beauty bells bloom!
A note from the charming blooms,
"May love find you at the beauty,
of dawn!"

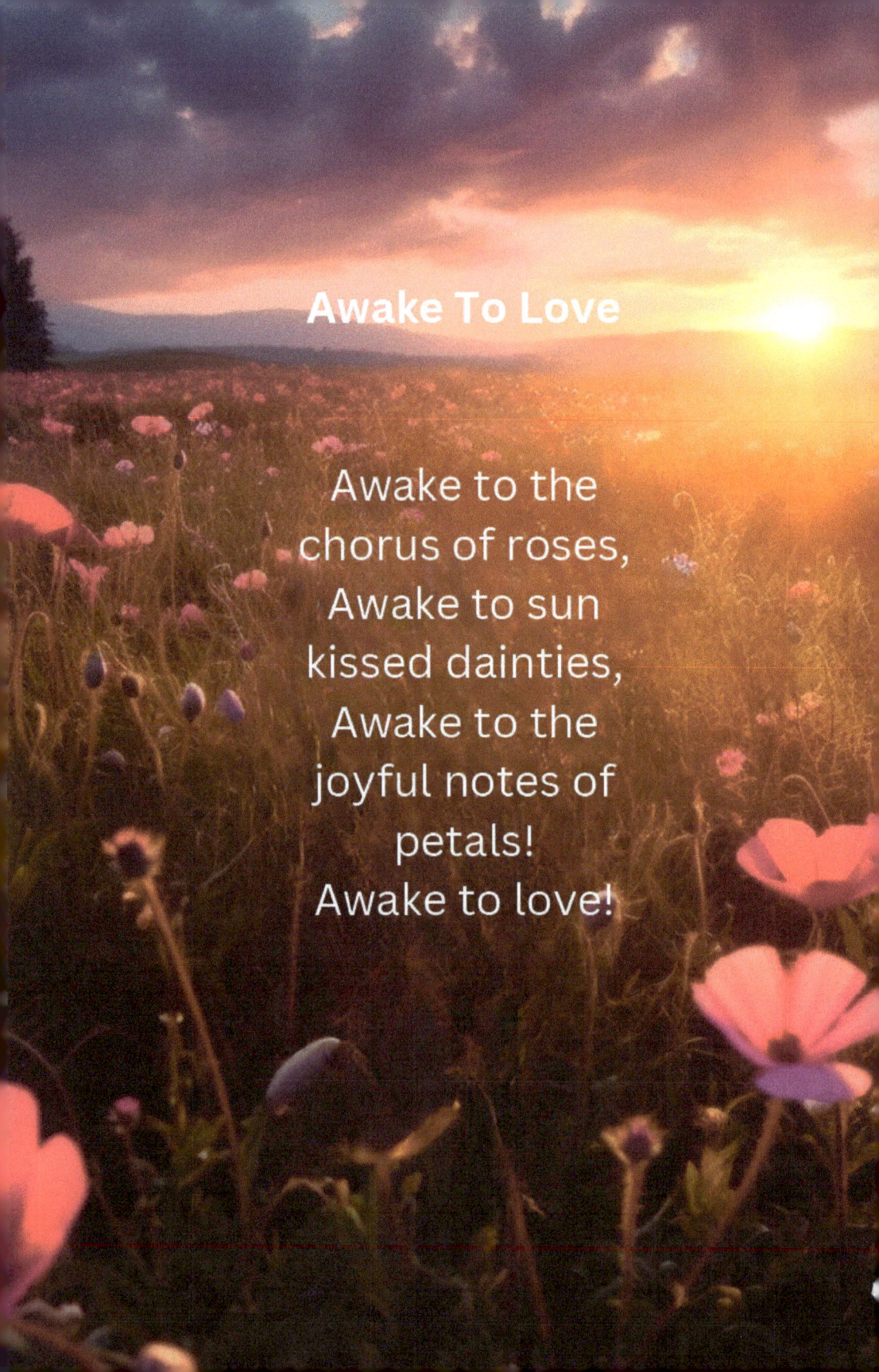

Awake To Love

Awake to the
chorus of roses,
Awake to sun
kissed dainties,
Awake to the
joyful notes of
petals!
Awake to love!

Beautified By Grace

Grace pours over me,
like fresh dew from
heaven;

I am empowered by love,
Beautified by grace!
Lifted by the Lord.

Beautiful Ground

May you walk on
beautiful grounds,
of love, lit with the
thriving notes of
floral blooms;
May profound joy,
be yours.

Beauty at Dawn

Beauty at dawn, bloomy and bright!
The echoes of a new day!
Whispers of new hopes unfolding!
The crackling sound of floral pods!
The reawakening, of floral joy!
The glistening dew, on petal tops;
The sparkles, and colourful notes
of joy, lights yet another day!

Beauty Flow
Love is a beautiful
flow of positivity,
that ignites care
and showers
affection.

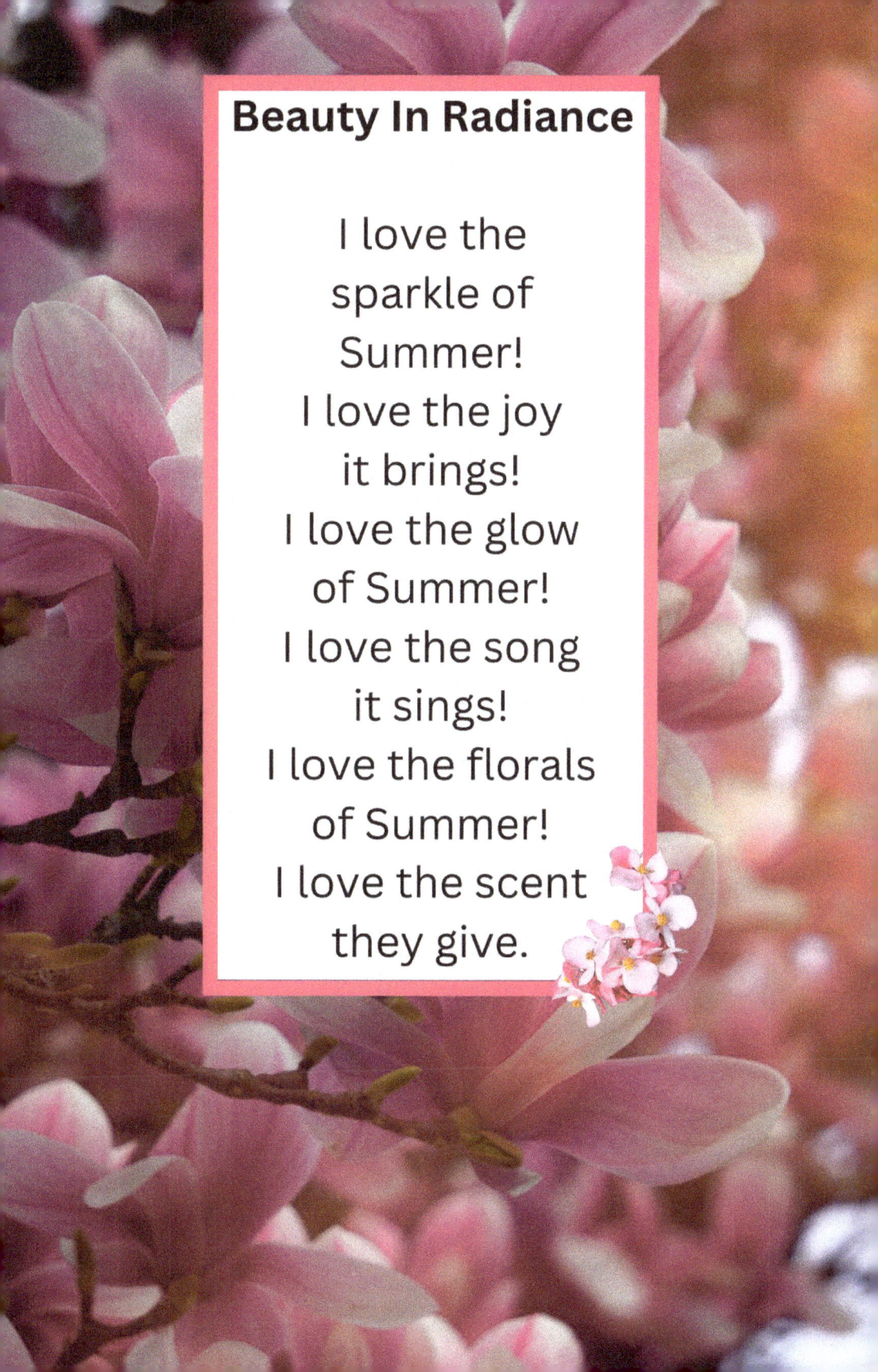

Beauty In Radiance

I love the
sparkle of
Summer!
I love the joy
it brings!
I love the glow
of Summer!
I love the song
it sings!
I love the florals
of Summer!
I love the scent
they give.

Beauty Of Nature

In the beauty
of nature,
His wonders,
are told!
His greatness,
is unfolded.

Beauty Sings

Joy blinks hope,
in the beauty of
radiant blooms;
Beauty sings in
the petals of,
flourishing
blooms!
There is a mist
of joy in the air,
hope rises as
new blooms!

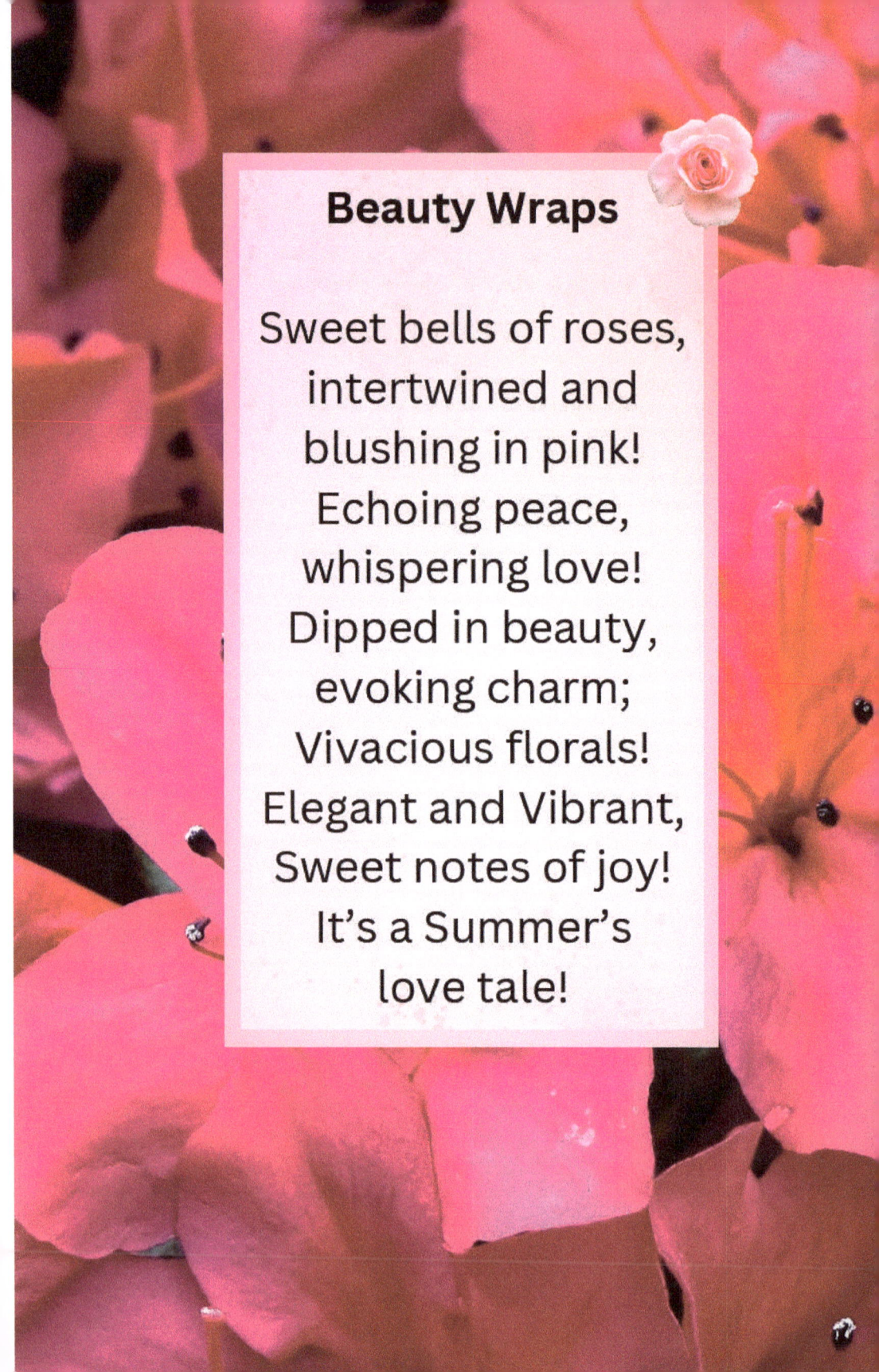

Beauty Wraps

Sweet bells of roses,
intertwined and
blushing in pink!
Echoing peace,
whispering love!
Dipped in beauty,
evoking charm;
Vivacious florals!
Elegant and Vibrant,
Sweet notes of joy!
It's a Summer's
love tale!

Blessings In Glow

Children are like flowers,
in the garden!
Tend to them, nurture them;
They will bloom beautifully,
and wrap you, in their love,
and affection.

Blooms Of Joy

Sweet dreamy
ranunculus, a joy
of radiant glow!
Awakes to beauty
in radiance!
A pride of the
Spring garden!
A joyful blend of
charming wonder.

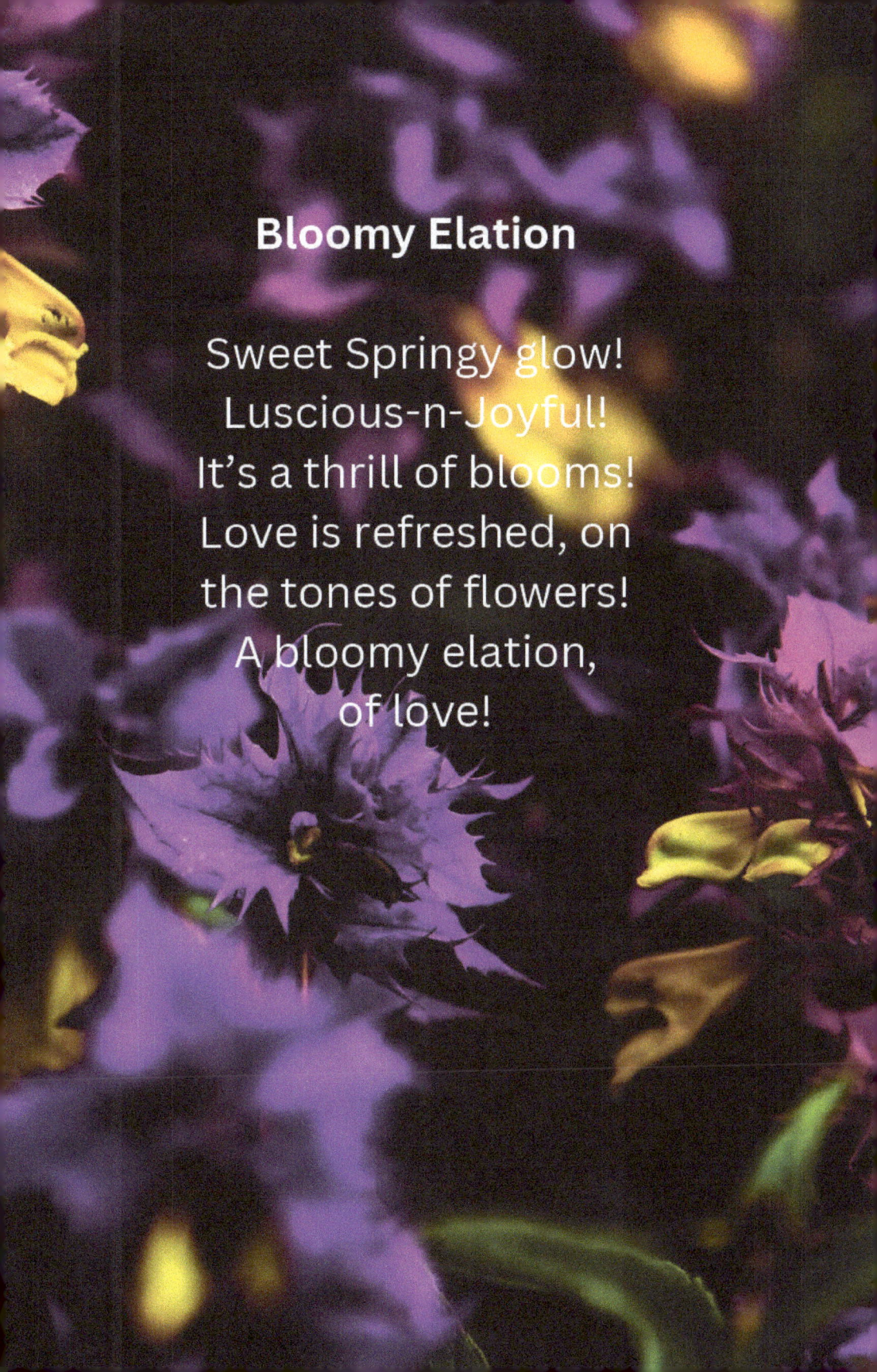

Bloomy Elation

Sweet Springy glow!
Luscious-n-Joyful!
It's a thrill of blooms!
Love is refreshed, on
the tones of flowers!
A bloomy elation,
of love!

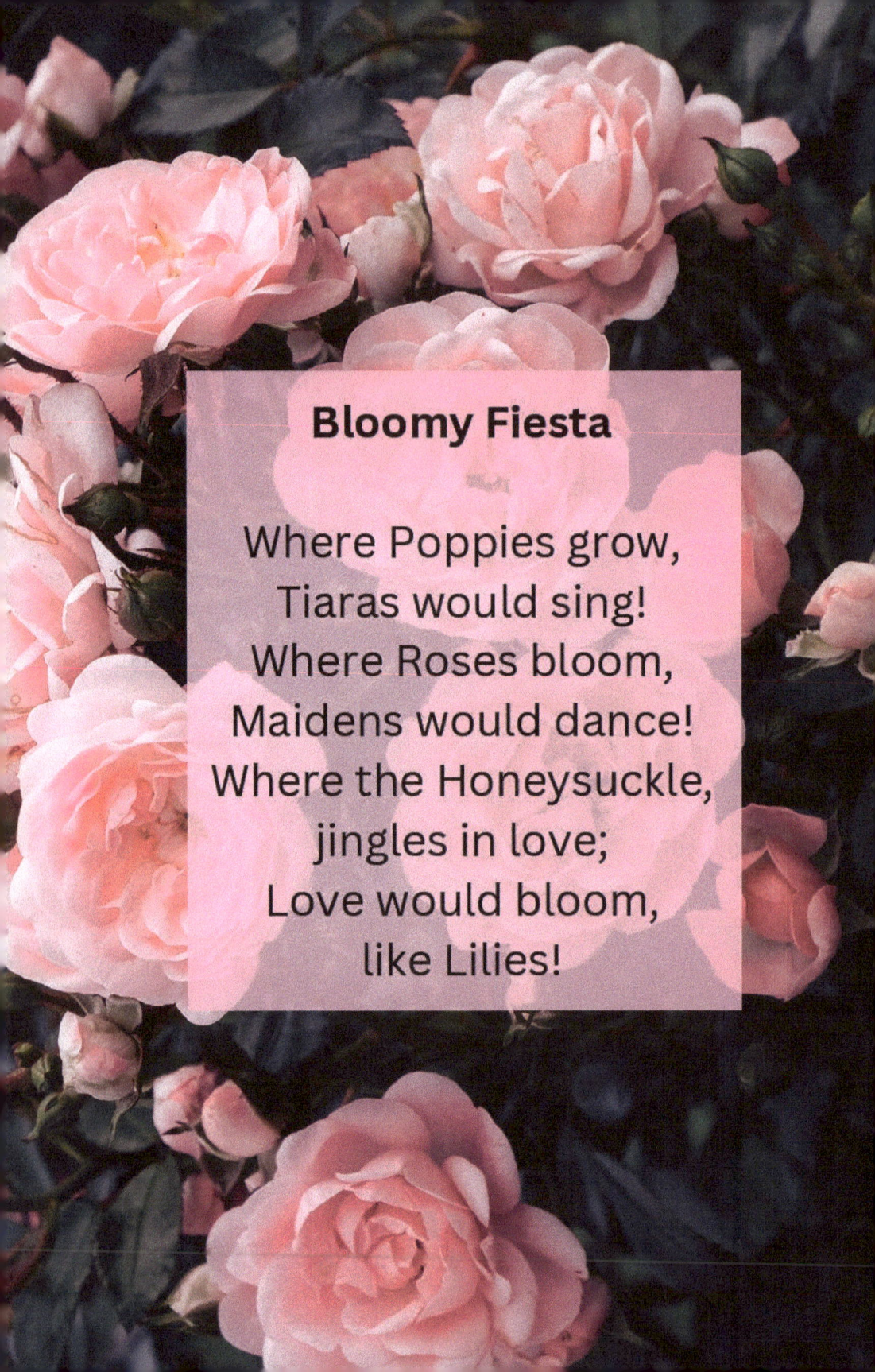

Bloomy Fiesta

Where Poppies grow,
Tiaras would sing!
Where Roses bloom,
Maidens would dance!
Where the Honeysuckle,
jingles in love;
Love would bloom,
like Lilies!

Bloomy Joy

It's a bloomy joy where the
flowers grow!
Glowing in the garden, like
crystals in the sun!
Glazed by love, lush, bountiful,
and joyful in bloom!
Singing in many colours!
Love sings in many ways!
In many colours!

Bloomy Wonder

She glows in sweet adoration!
Love is ignited in bloomy glow!
Flourishing in beauty,
It's the sparkles, that makes
the "Rose," a bloomy wonder!

Blossom in Favor

May you, blossom in the favor of the Lord, in all beauty, and radiance.

Cocktail Of Love

It's a cocktail of love, when
blooms come together,
in sweet harmony, spicing
up the garden!
It's a cocktail of joy, when
praises are harmoniously,
lifted to the Lord!

Colour Me

Colour me pearl, in love and elegance!
Colour me joyfully, in refreshing tones,
Colour me vibrant, on a rainbow day!
Colour me purple, in draping beauty!
Colour me gold, in alluring beauty.

Cover Me

Embrace me with
Your mercies!
Cover me with
Your love!
Shield me with
Your favor!
O Great Lord!

Daisy Blooms

Sweet daisies
tucked in tunes,
of bloomy beauty!
Dipped in joyful
tones of calm!
Like a Taaffeite!
Like a Sapphire!
in flourishing
bloom!
It's a pearly garden,
of gemstones!

Dance Of Jewels

It's a joyful day!
It's a peaceful
time!
The whispers of
blooms!
The joyful notes
of roses!
The clapping of
petals!
All praising the
name of the
Lord!

Dandelions-A-Glow

Dandelions-a-glow, radiance in bloom,
Dandelions-a-glow, ringing in joy!
Dandelions-a-glow, hope renewed!
Dandelions-a-glow, on the rolling hills!
Dandelions-a-glow, wishes are made,
on the whispering fields;
Dandelions-a-glow, beauty refreshed!
Dandelions-a-glow, in glow!

Dawn Rises

Dawn rises to the
unveiling of hope,
on floral notes;
with a song of joy!
Joy will arise at
the break of dawn,
with a melody!

Dawn Unfolds

Precious are the bountiful floral notes of the roses, "Sweet and Fruity" warming hearts, evoking joy!

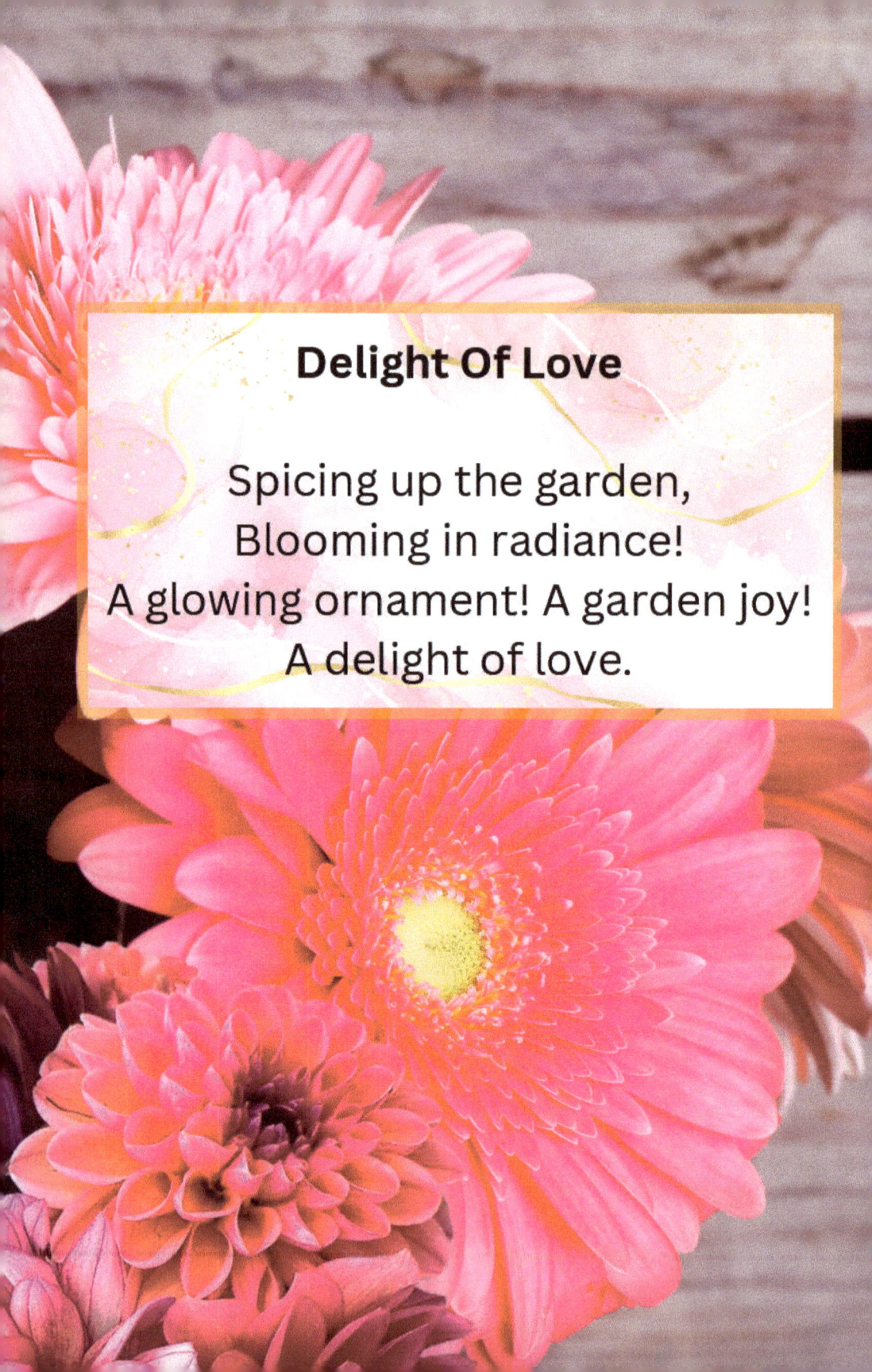

Delight Of Love

Spicing up the garden,
Blooming in radiance!
A glowing ornament! A garden joy!
A delight of love.

Dressed In Love

Love paints everyone gold!
Declares everyone free!
Dresses everyone beautiful.

Drips and Dips

Joy unfolds in the
beauty of many
colours;
Love is a colourful
experience of joy.

Echoing Beauty

Opening up to the
golden glow
the rose dazzles,
with an echoing
beauty of joy!
It's a wonder
world.

Enveloping In Warmth

Love is a
precious gift,
enveloping in
warmth and joy.

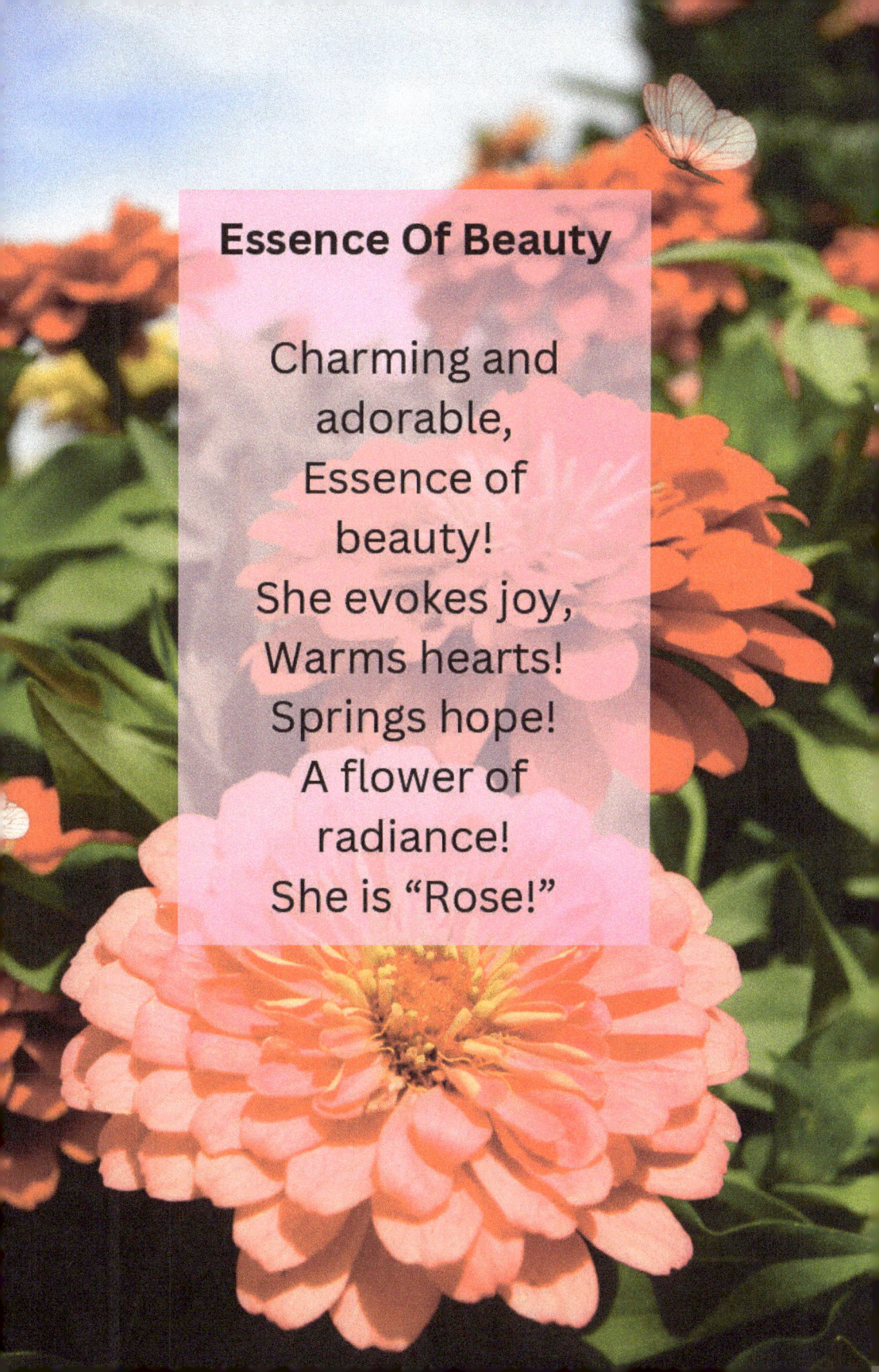

Essence Of Beauty

Charming and
adorable,
Essence of
beauty!
She evokes joy,
Warms hearts!
Springs hope!
A flower of
radiance!
She is "Rose!"

Fancy World

It's a rosey fancy
world,
Frilly roses dance,
to the joyful wind,
It's a rosey juicy
flow, where the
bees hangout.
It's a rosy glow,
that lights the
garden, where
love blooms
as flowers.

Festal Dance

A festal dance of blooms,
A sweet recount of,
tender mercies!
A joyful acclamation of,
His, love!
Sweet songs of grace!
Blooming in floral joy!

Floral Chandelier

Sweet floral chandelier,
hanging up the tree!
Like a lamp softly glowing,
lending rays to the garden!
A golden lit glow of love,
unfolding sweet accords!
Let the roses thrill you with
heart-warming notes!

Floral Courts

It's an endless stream of floral
bloom, in "Love's Palace,"
It's an endless bubble of joy,
in the floral courts!
It's an endless beauty sparkle,
in bloomy land.

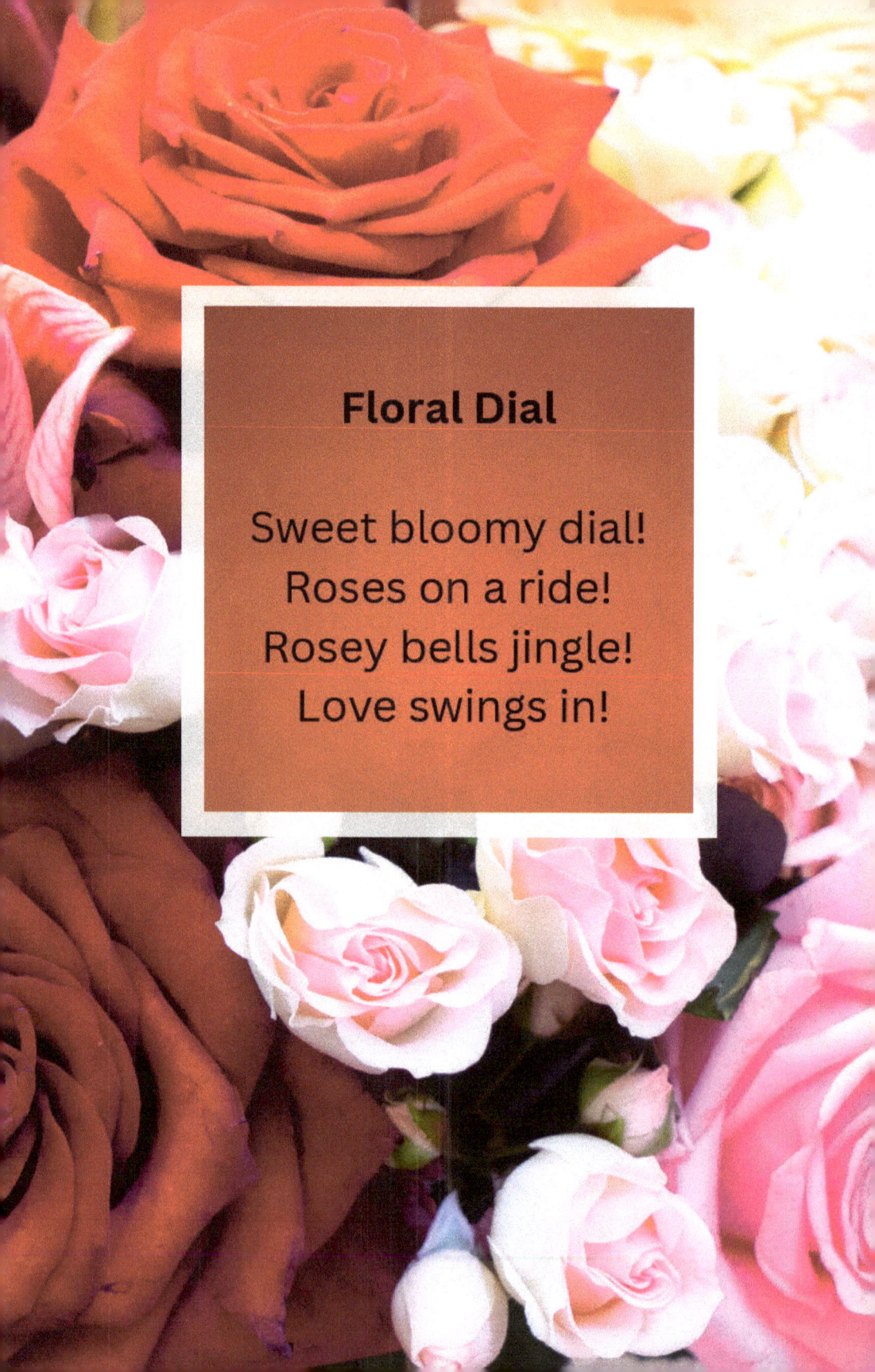

Floral Dial

Sweet bloomy dial!
Roses on a ride!
Rosey bells jingle!
Love swings in!

Floral Echoes

It's a joyful return of
florals in Spring!
A whimsy dance of floral
bridals in Summer!
A bountiful floral splash
in Fall!
It's all floral rhapsody
in Winter!

Floral Notes

Beautiful are
the notes of florals,
Lovely are
the rhythms of
its love!
Full
of inspiration,
love, and joy.

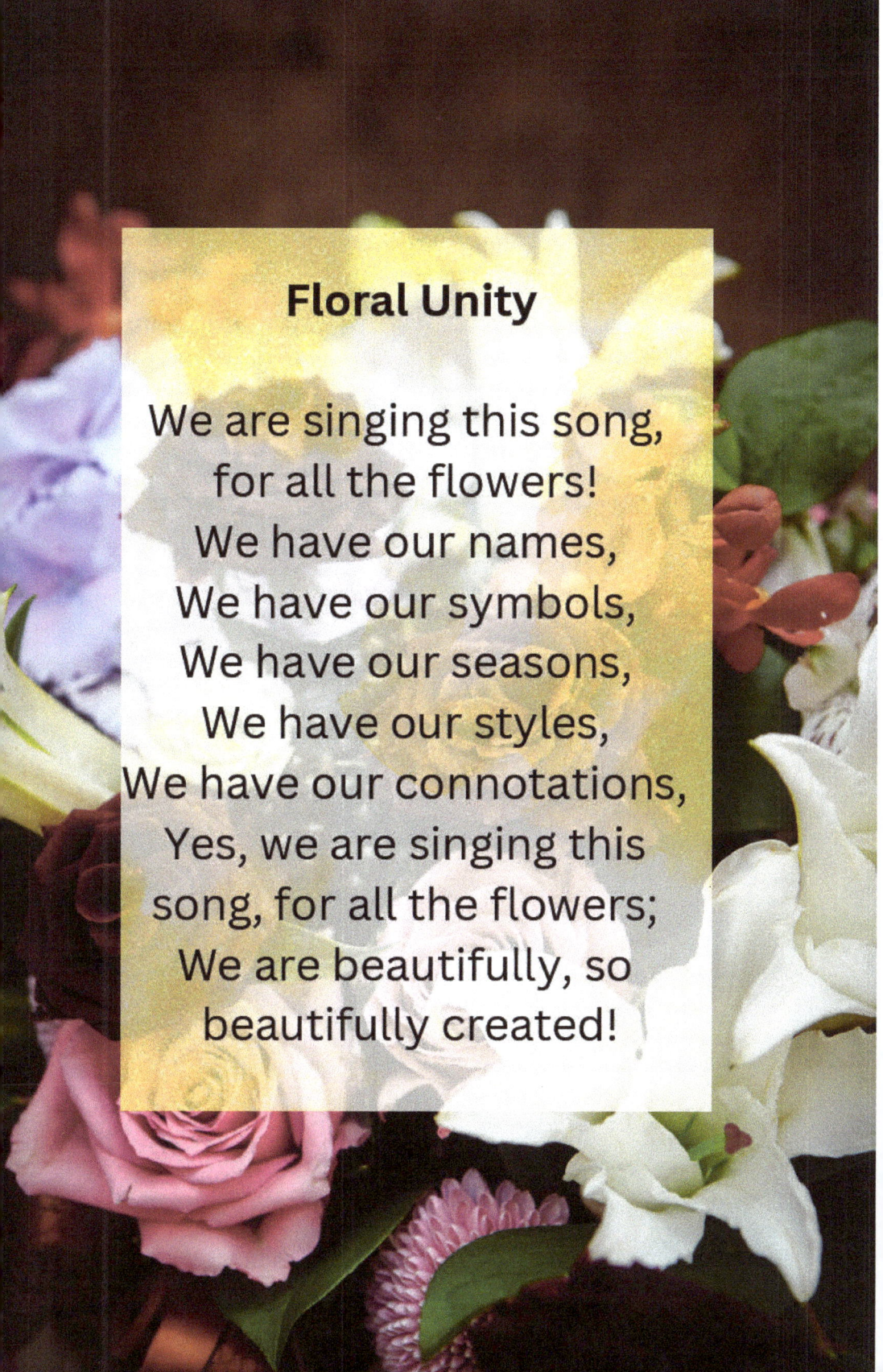

Floral Unity

We are singing this song,
for all the flowers!
We have our names,
We have our symbols,
We have our seasons,
We have our styles,
We have our connotations,
Yes, we are singing this
song, for all the flowers;
We are beautifully, so
beautifully created!

Flourishing Gems

Flowers are blooming again!
The meadows turn green,
Birds are heard singing,
Melody and joy fills the air!
It's the awakening of a new season;
The bells chime peace, all is well.

Flower Agates

Crystallized in bloomy beauty!
A sweet floral charming moment,
It's a joyful touch of whimsy glow!
A joyous rhythm of rising blooms!
Nature heard it all, it's all floral
glam, where the roses grow!

Flower In My Hand

Love placed a flower, in my hand.
Its notes are warm, and cheery;
Its fragrance is very alluring!
Love placed a flower, in my hand.
Forever fresh!
Forever mine!

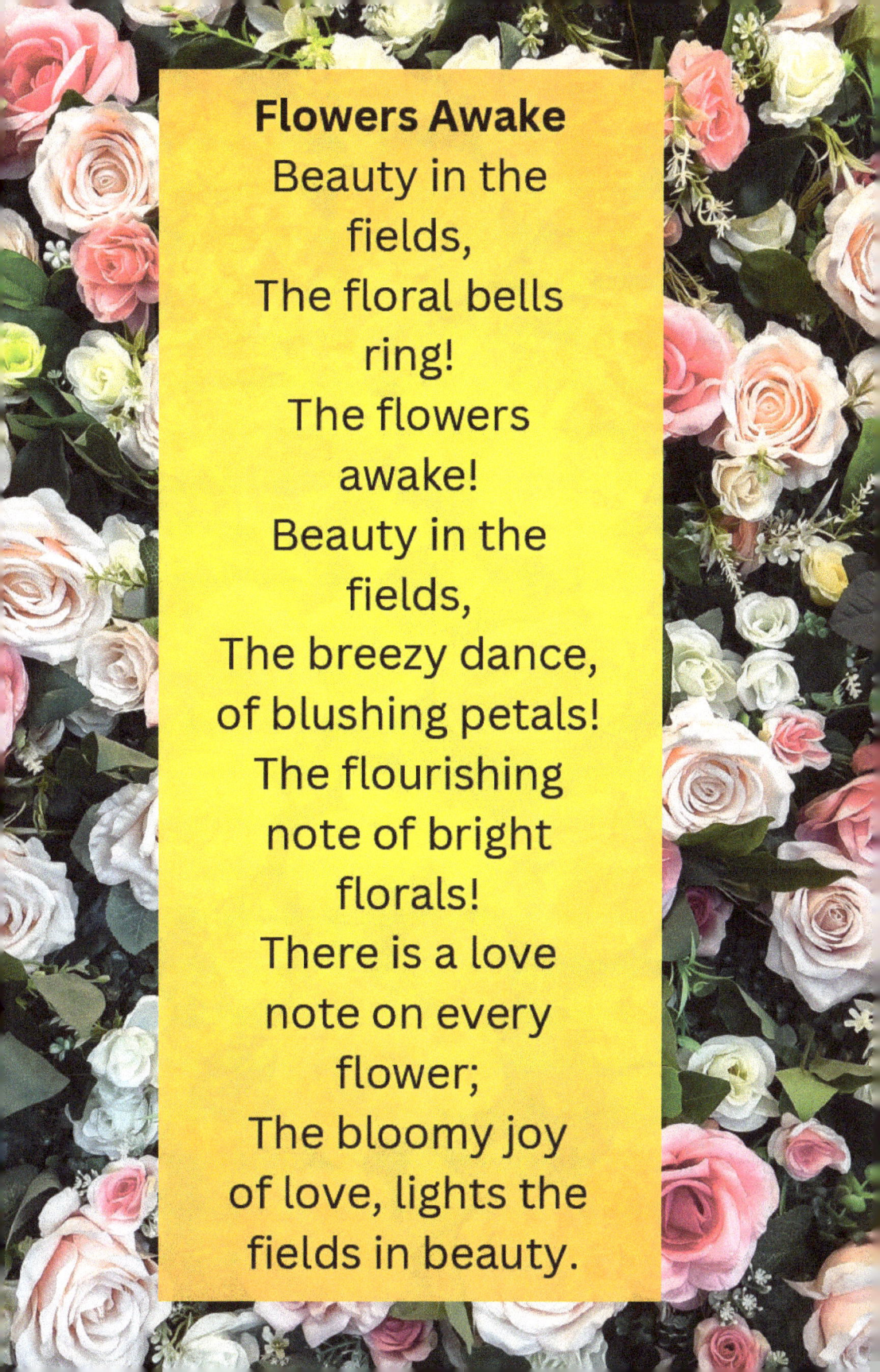

Flowers Awake

Beauty in the fields,
The floral bells ring!
The flowers awake!
Beauty in the fields,
The breezy dance,
of blushing petals!
The flourishing note of bright florals!
There is a love note on every flower;
The bloomy joy of love, lights the fields in beauty.

Fresh Mercies

Fresh mercies bloom everyday beautifully, with an aura of favor!

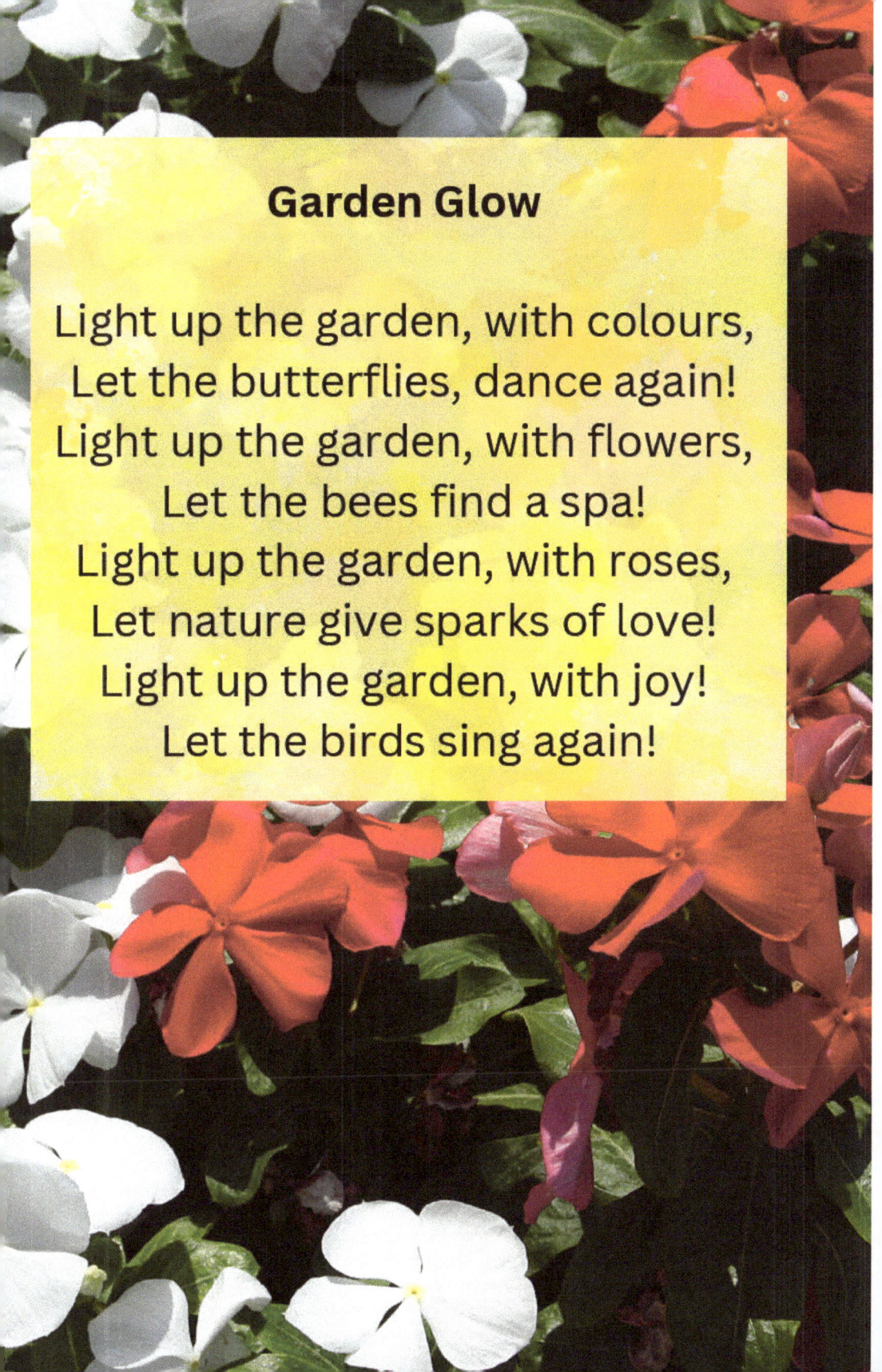

Garden Glow

Light up the garden, with colours,
Let the butterflies, dance again!
Light up the garden, with flowers,
Let the bees find a spa!
Light up the garden, with roses,
Let nature give sparks of love!
Light up the garden, with joy!
Let the birds sing again!

Garden Joy

Let's make life a
beautiful garden!
Let's make life a
scented garden,
where flowers
bloom in love! Let's show care,
Let love be our
fragrance!
Let's pray for one
another, help one
another, cherish
one another;
Let's blossom in,
love, peace, and joy!

Gates Of Dawn

May joy find you at,
the gates of dawn!
When the morning
glow comes, may
peace be yours;
May love bubble,
with new colours
of joy your way!
May beauty be
yours.

Glaze Of Beauty

There is a glaze of beauty,
in the sky!
Like a sparkle,
of diamond,
A new dawn unfolds,
Marvelous are the,
works of the Lord;
Creation sings his,
greatness!
He is Lord, over all.

Glow Preciously

Daisies whisper
new beginnings,
Roses echo love,
Glow in the Lord's
goodness!

Glowing Gemstones

Like a Pink Zircon
gemstone, the
sun glows in love,
and beauty!
It's a Kunzite,
hanging in joy!
Sparkling like a
Rose de France
amethyst;
The sun flashes,
vibrant colours,
of harmony!

Golden Glow

Oh golden sun! you blink your eyes,
and the colours come flashing;
Colours that are warm and spicy!
Colours that are vibrant and
charming!
Golden colours exuding joy,
Bright colours promising hope,
Beautiful colours radiating
positivity,
Joyful colours embracing life;
You shine in radiance!
You brighten the day!

Golden Moments

May you walk
in the glowing
rhythm of joy!
May your path,
be filled with
the flashing
notes of florals,
lit with golden
moments.

Golden Rhythms

Golden rhythms
of joy,
Sweet accords,
of roses,
Love blows its,
trumpets!

Grace Flows

Favor Shines,
Mercy Glows!
At
The Pinnacle of Grace.

Graceful Abundance

Beauty-n-Glow!
Like a star in
the garden,
Shimmering in
beauty!
May you shine
with radiance!
May you touch
the world, with
glowing love.

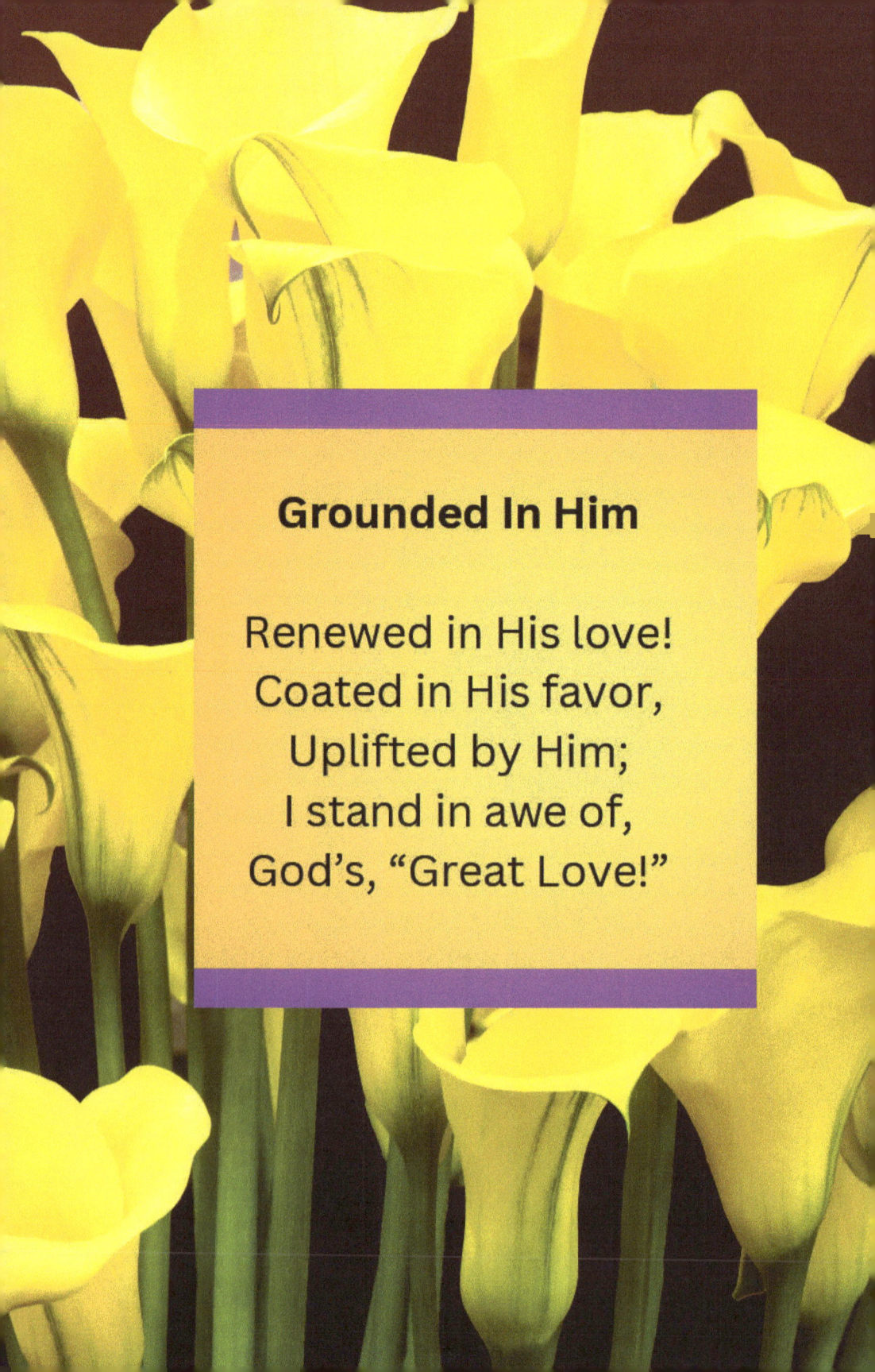

Grounded In Him

Renewed in His love!
Coated in His favor,
Uplifted by Him;
I stand in awe of,
God's, "Great Love!"

He Answers

Don't cry in the garden,
where the flowers grow;
Don't cry in the garden,
where the lilies sing!
Don't cry in the garden,
where the roses bloom:
Just sing His name!
Sing His praise!
He answers prayers.

He Cares

When the glow is gone,
and the night time comes,
just remember, He shines
through the darkness;
Jesus is LORD!
When the smiles are gone,
and the tears roll down;
just remember, He cares!
Jesus is LOVE!
When you feel lost and
alone, just remember,
He is a faithful friend,
Jesus is LOVE!
When you have missed
the way, and all seems
bleak, just remember,
He is always, by your side,
He is the "WAY"
Jesus is LORD!

He Is Great
Let us come into His presence,
knowing and believing;
He does things great and mighty!
He does things no one else, can do.

Hope Blooms

Hope blooms like a flower, springing forth in due time to the joy of beauty, and reality.

Hope Renewed

Hope is renewed,
at the birth of;
a new dawn!

I Hear

I hear whispers, from the passing wind,
I hear the melody of birds!
I hear joyous rhythms, in the air;
I hear the voices of children, playing,
in the garden!

I open my petals,
praising Him,
who has made;
all things,
beautiful!!

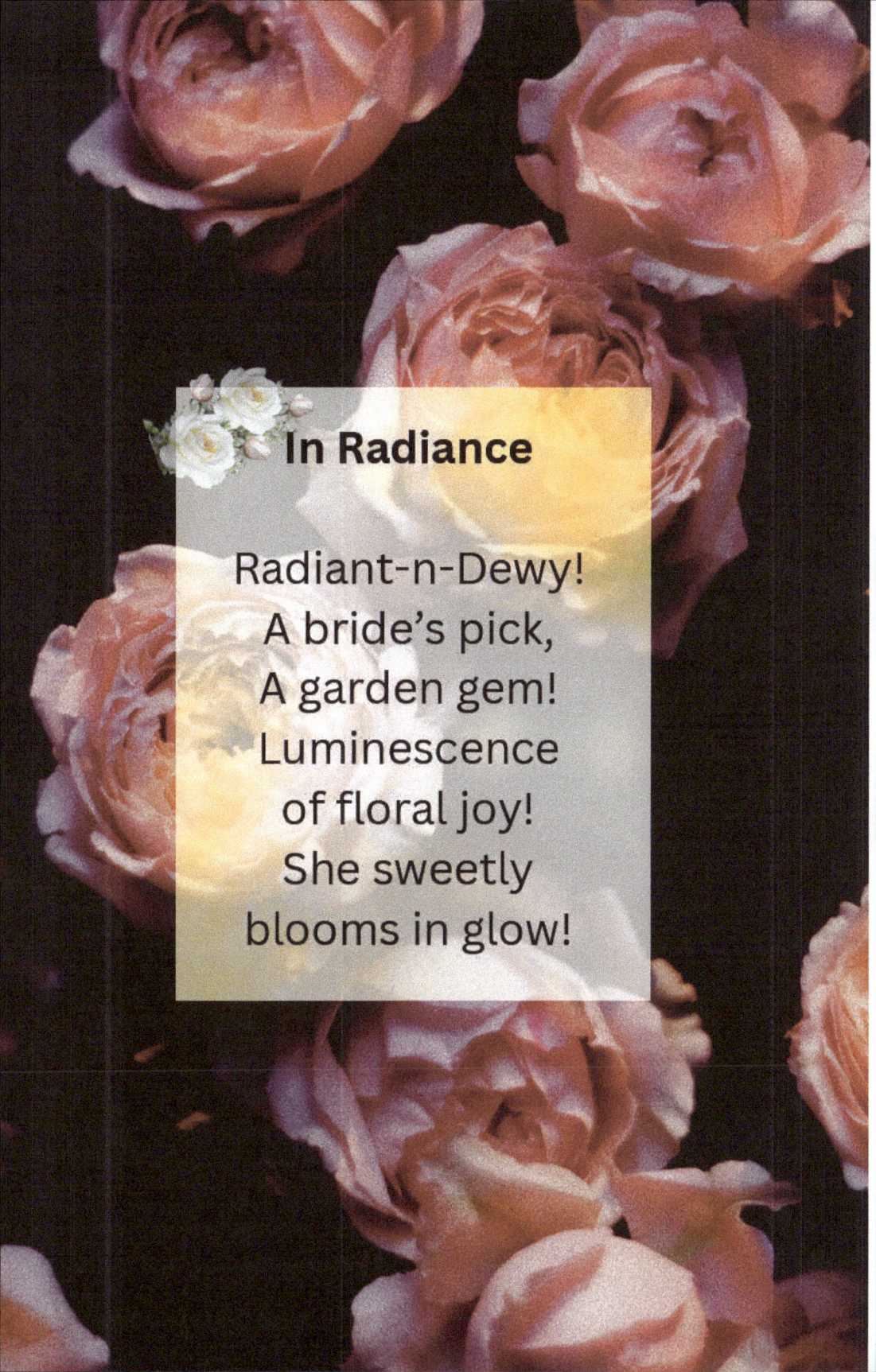

In Radiance

Radiant-n-Dewy!
A bride's pick,
A garden gem!
Luminescence
of floral joy!
She sweetly
blooms in glow!

Isles Of Love

Through the corridors of time!
Through the isles of love!
Through the glazy sea of love!
Through the bloomy pathway!
The "Rose" walks through,
as an allegory of love!

It's A Feeling

It's a feeling of joy that energizes,
It's a feeling of care that pacifies,
It's a feeling of love that beautifies,
It's a feeling of grace that restores,
It's a feeling of hope that assures,
It's a feeling of peace that calms.

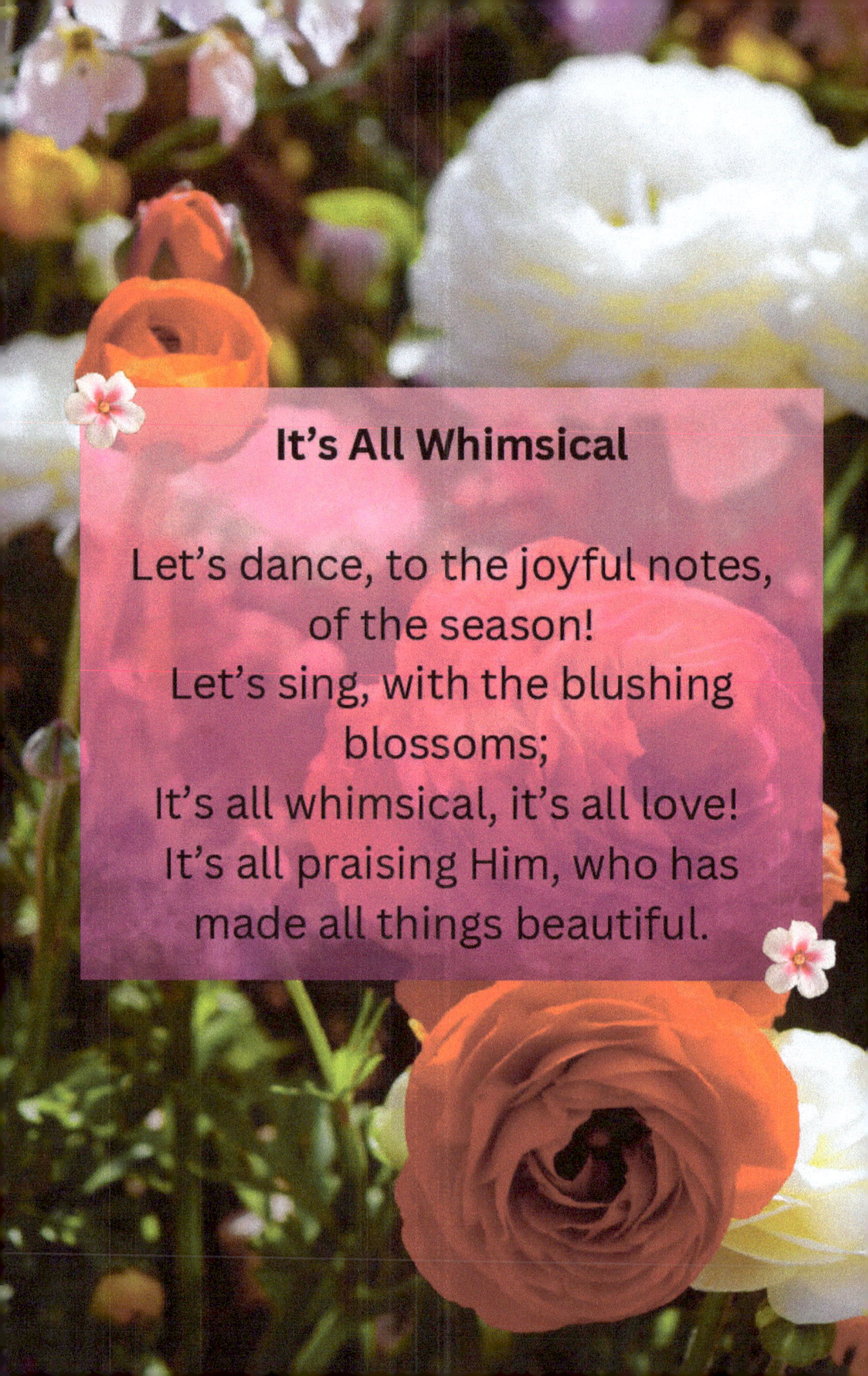

It's All Whimsical

Let's dance, to the joyful notes,
of the season!
Let's sing, with the blushing
blossoms;
It's all whimsical, it's all love!
It's all praising Him, who has
made all things beautiful.

Jewels Of Radiance

Jewels of the garden!
Ornaments of the fields,
Bouquets of comfort!
Bloomy charms of joy!

Joan's Garden

In Joan's garden,
they spring forth, in radiance!
Sweet cornets of Roses!
Flamboyant in bloomy beauty!
Pearls of the garden, a gift of love!
A reminiscence of hope,
A flow of joy! A toast to love!

In Joan's garden,
Sweet tunes play out, in memory
of those gone by!
Roses in dainty pink!
Sing in floral fiesta, in joyful notes!
A sweet tale of love!

In Joan's garden,
Beauty is reborn!
A dawn of joy!
An evocation of love!
A world of beauty!
An oasis of peace!

Joy Of Friendship

Friends are like a bouquet of flowers, placed in our hands, with each variety, representing a meaning, adding colour, and exuding joy!

Joyful Bloom

"Joyful, Joyful, Bloom,"
Humming beauty, in bleak times;
Singing joy, whispering love!
It's "Rose," the beauty at dawn.

Joyful Echoes

It's a new breath of delight!
A new show of love,
New colours of joy!
May beauty always come,
your way!

Joyful Flow

Knit in His love!
Bond in His,
grace!
In shawls of
favor, may
you be covered
everyday!

Joyful Reveal

Every opening of
the flower,
Is a revelation
of beauty,
divinely placed;
uniquely created!

Joyful Springs

In colourful
springs of
joy,
Love flows!

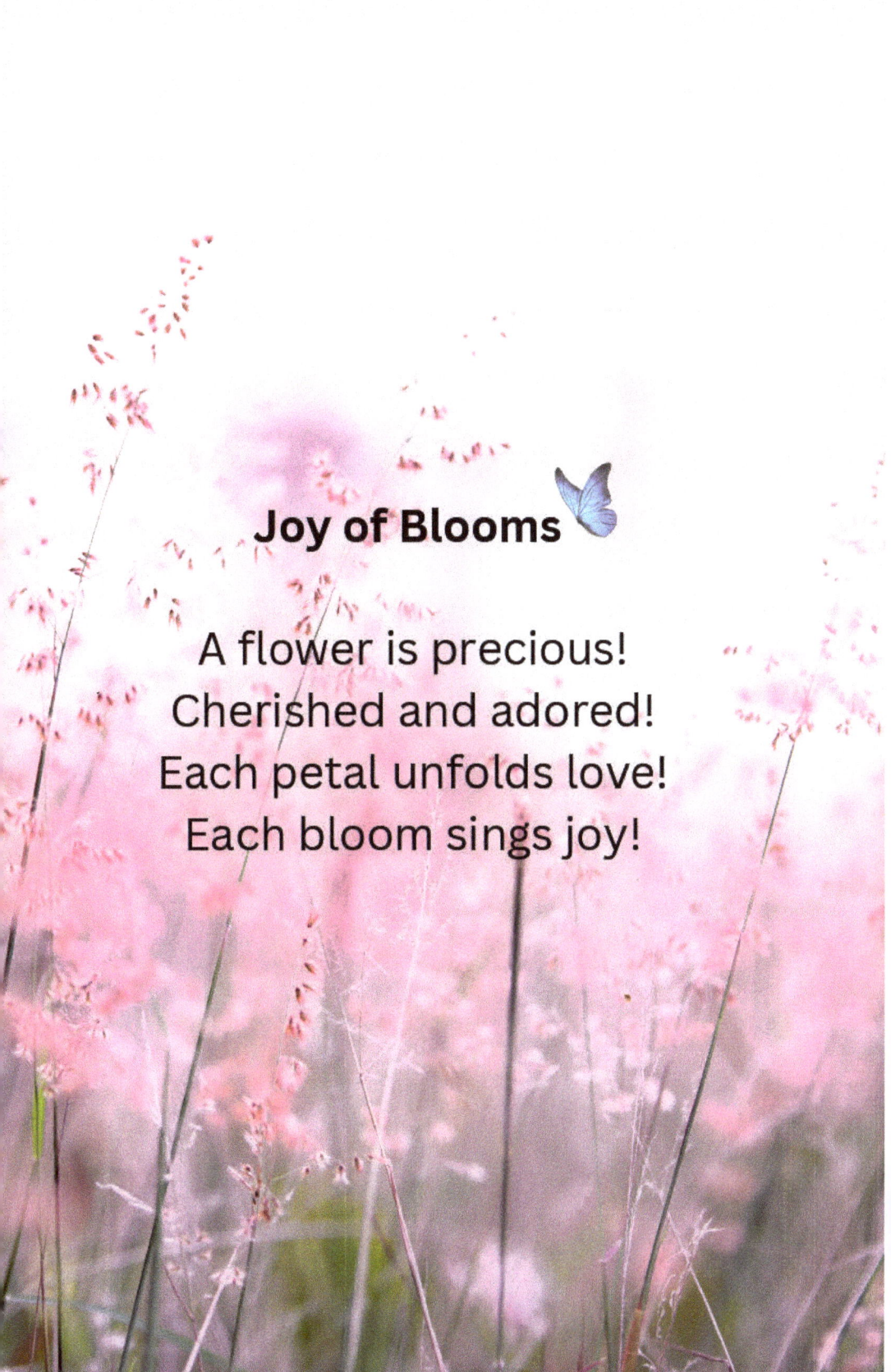

Joy of Blooms

A flower is precious!
Cherished and adored!
Each petal unfolds love!
Each bloom sings joy!

Knit In Love

We are knit in love
petals in bloom!
We are bond in love
florals of radiance!
We have different
goals and outlooks!
We have different
colours and styles!
We come unified
in cause,
We come
together to make
the world a
beautiful place!

Lady Of Joy

Like a lady in waiting,
She glows in beauty
She illumines the garden
with positivity,
She exudes warmth,
She radiates love!
She is a lady of joy!
She is precious!

Lady Petunia

Where the floral
gems dwell,
The "Lady Petunia"
swings in!
Whispering love,
with rhythms that
gladden the heart.

Let It Come

Let it come flowing over you!
Let it come as dew drops, on the
mountain top!
Let it come freshly over you!
The goodness of the Lord!
The beauty of the Lord!
Let it come!

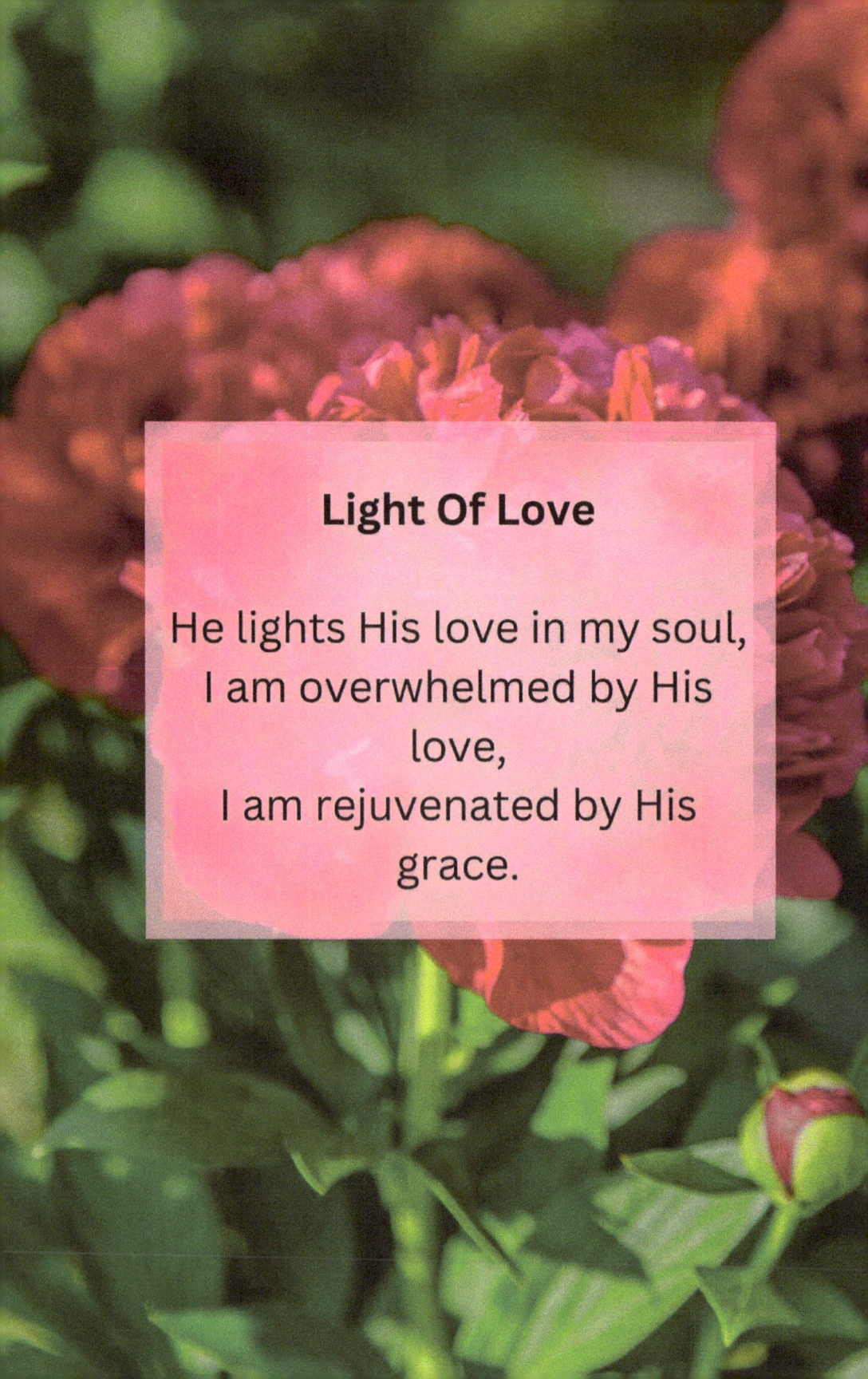

Light Of Love

He lights His love in my soul,
I am overwhelmed by His
love,
I am rejuvenated by His
grace.

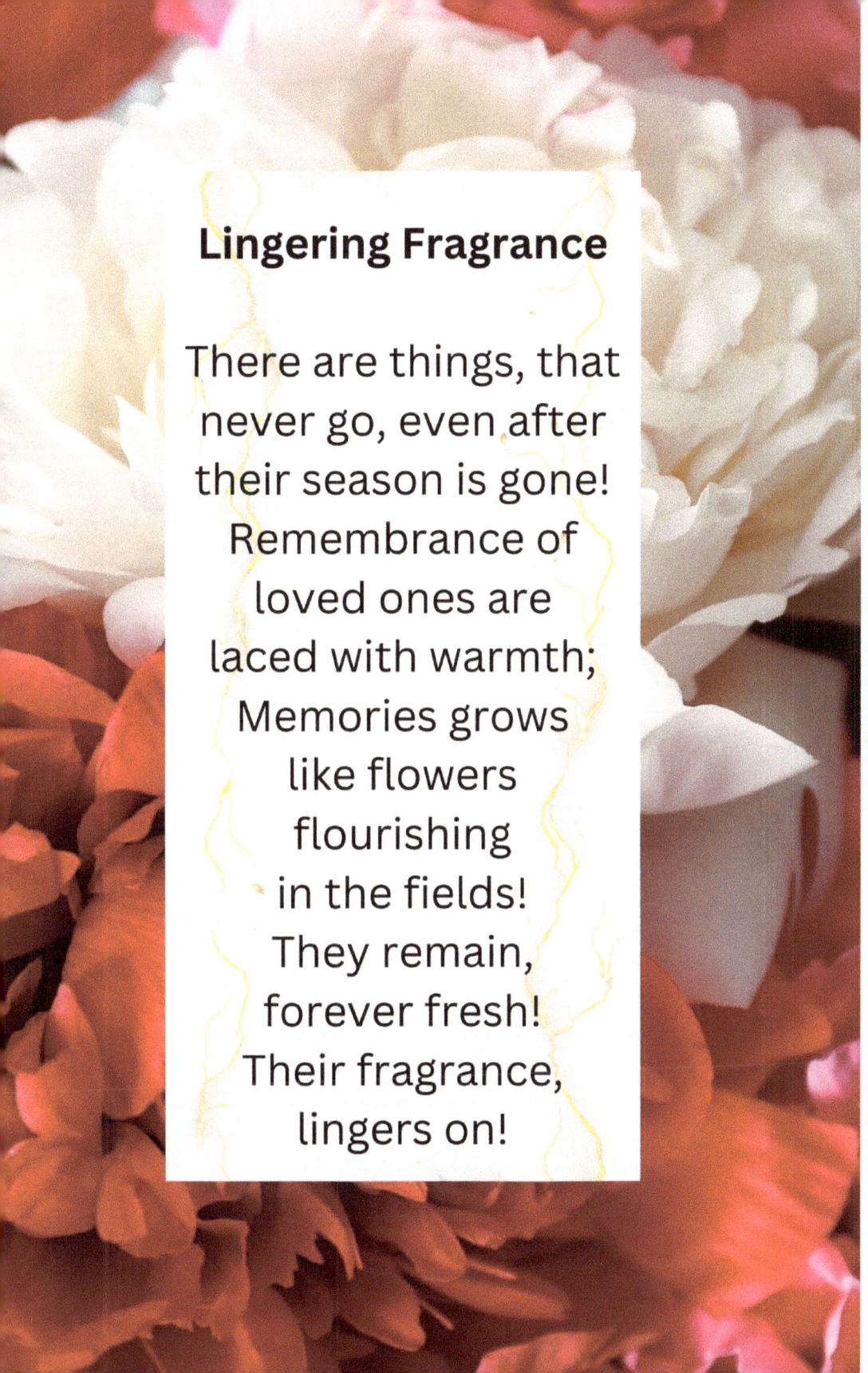

Lingering Fragrance

There are things, that
never go, even after
their season is gone!
Remembrance of
loved ones are
laced with warmth;
Memories grows
like flowers
flourishing
in the fields!
They remain,
forever fresh!
Their fragrance,
lingers on!

Love And Kindness

Memories are like,
butterflies dancing,
in cold air!
It is love that gives,
them warmth
and a place in our
hearts.

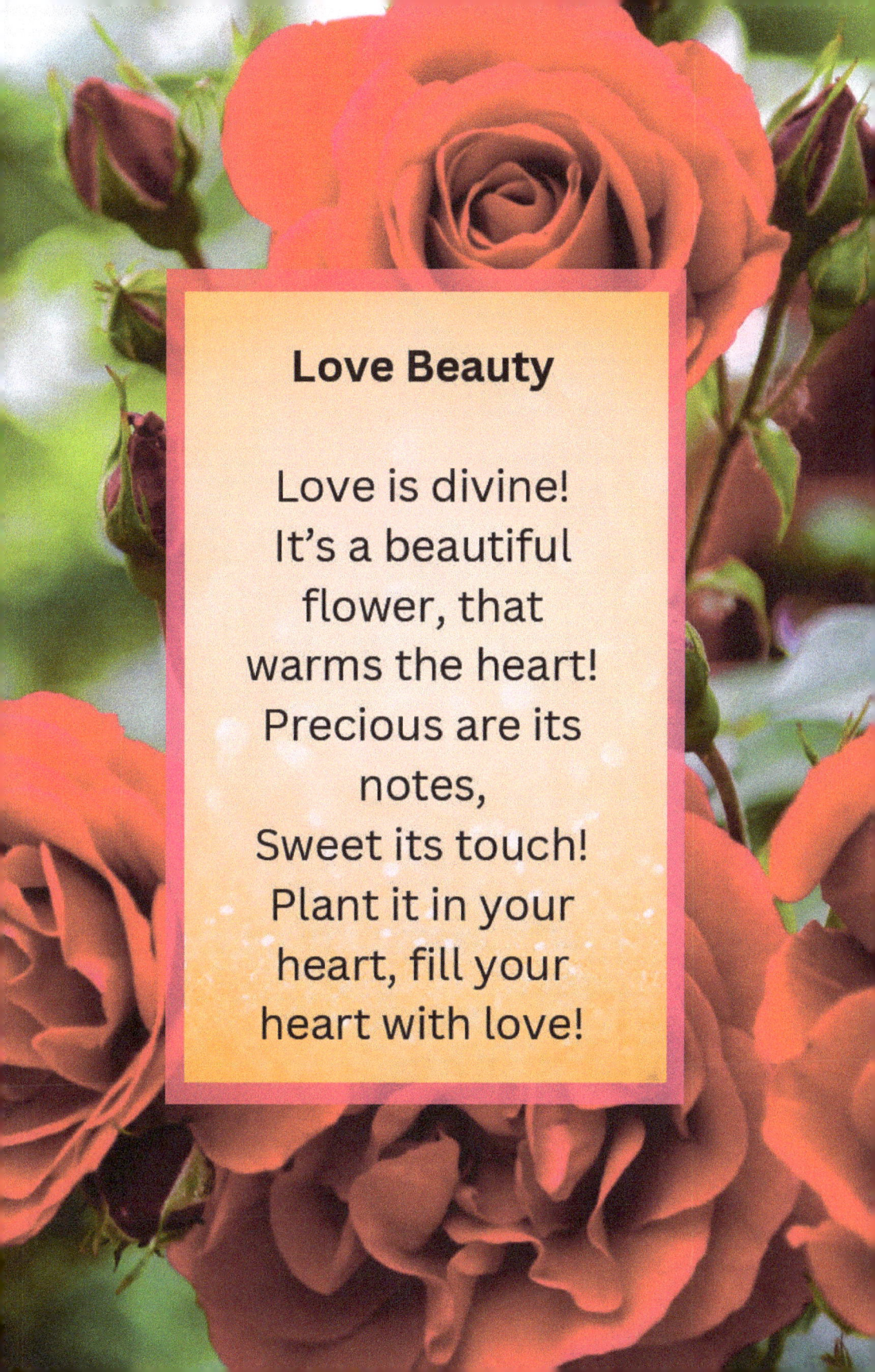

Love Beauty

Love is divine!
It's a beautiful
flower, that
warms the heart!
Precious are its
notes,
Sweet its touch!
Plant it in your
heart, fill your
heart with love!

Love Blooms

Love blooms
like a flower!
Nurture it, and
let it wrap you,
in the
sweetness
of its
fragrance!

Love Goes On

Love goes on singing,
glowing, and painting,
hearts with gold!

Love Ignited

Whispers from the dainty blooms,
"Love ignited, Love renewed,"
"Love blossoming bright,"
On a beautiful sunny day!

Love Is A Beautiful Song

Love is a beautiful song, when in tune;
"With the rhythms of the wind!"
"With the floral notes, of the roses"
"With the vocals of the oscines"
"With the chorus of the wood trush!"
"With the songs of the starlings"
Love is a beautiful song, when sang;
in tune with the rhythms, of our hearts!

Love Nest

I grow in love,
I am touched,
by love!
I thrive in love!
I am beautified,
by love.

Love Notes

Love plays me a
fiddle, in May!
Love plays me a
fiddle, where the
dandelions have
found a home!
Love plays me a
fiddle, where the
butterflies dance,
and hop in search
of liquid gold!
Love plays me a
fiddle, when all
else is quiet.

Love Our Song

Let love be our song,
Let beauty be our symbol,
As we blossom beautifully,
In a world lit with love!

Love Story

The greatest love story, is the story, of the, "Cross."

Love Touch

Touch the world, with love, let the
flowers grow!
Touch the world, with love, let the
children sing!
Touch the world, with love, show
someone you care.

Love's Gate

At love's gate beauty spins a song!
A melody of hope warming the
heart,
A rhythm of calm, energizing, and
ushering us into blissful moments;
At love's gate the flowers sing
again.

Love's Island

Love on a sunny
island,
The tinker bells ring!
Love in a beautiful
garden,
The honey birds
sing!
Love in a lush
garden,
The bees have
found a home!
Love on a lovely
day,
The roses come
blooming,
Love glows with a tint of pink!

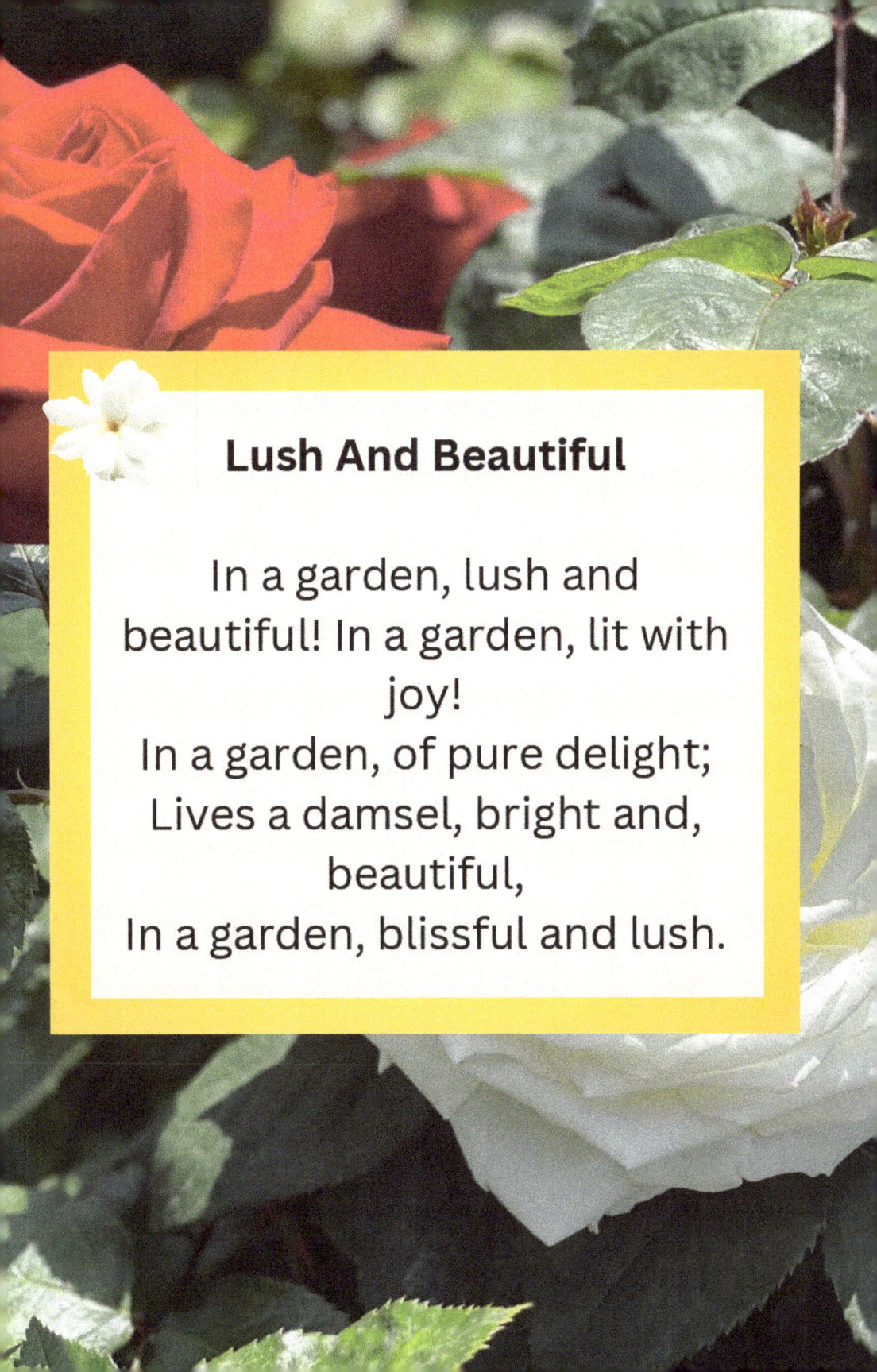

Lush And Beautiful

In a garden, lush and beautiful! In a garden, lit with joy!
In a garden, of pure delight;
Lives a damsel, bright and, beautiful,
In a garden, blissful and lush.

Lyrics of Roses

Love
sings with the lyrics, of
the roses;
In tunes, that gladden,
the heart.

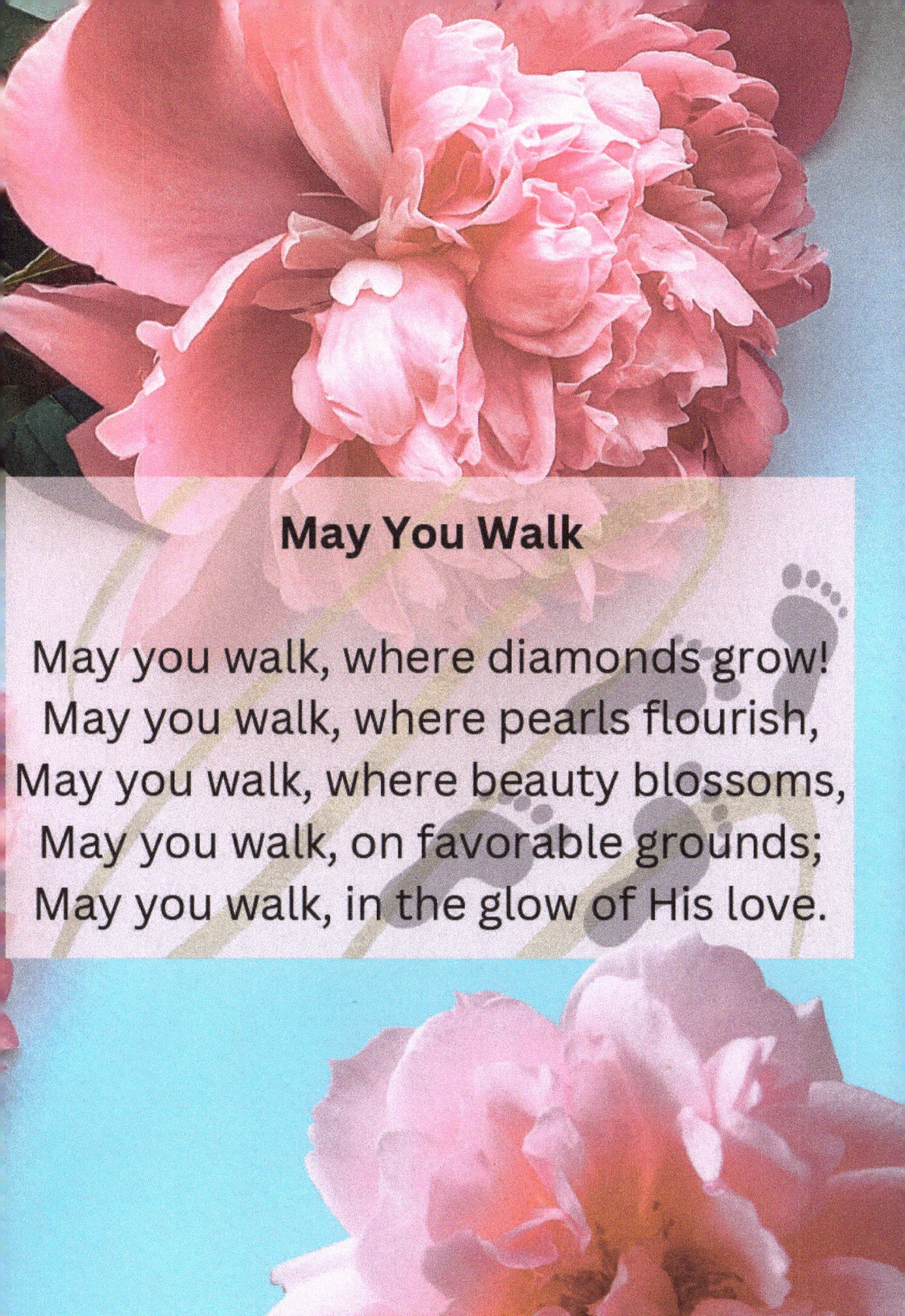

May You Walk

May you walk, where diamonds grow!
May you walk, where pearls flourish,
May you walk, where beauty blossoms,
May you walk, on favorable grounds;
May you walk, in the glow of His love.

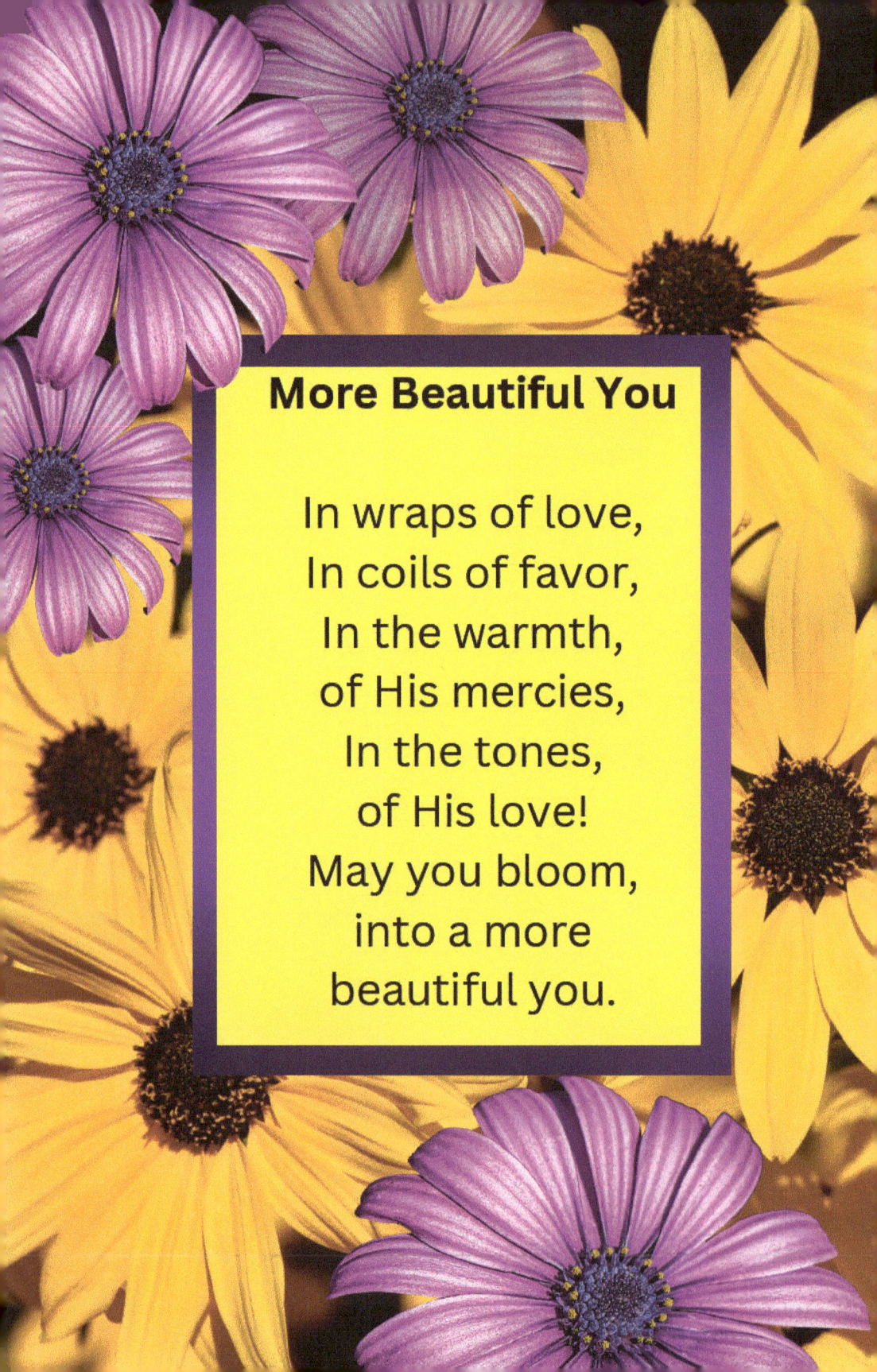

More Beautiful You

In wraps of love,
In coils of favor,
In the warmth,
of His mercies,
In the tones,
of His love!
May you bloom,
into a more
beautiful you.

Nature's Reveal

Nature opens
its curtains,
revealing
beauty
echoing love.

New Day

In His grace find
strength!
In His love find joy!
In His mercies find
renewal,
In His promises,
find hope.

New Notes

New notes are written,
Fresh calls of grace!
It's the unwrapping of,
petals!
It's the unfolding of,
love!

Not Alone

Growing in the field, but not alone!
Growing in the field, but still cared
for;
Growing in the field, but still loved!
God watches over all,
He has created!

Notes Of Love

Sweet fragrant,
notes of love!
Rubies in glow!
Roses in bloom,
A bountiful gift!
A timeless,
treasure.

On Petal Strings

On petal strings!
Beauty is found,
Love is laced,
Joy is knit!
In the beauty,
of petal strings.

Open The Curtains

Do not shut out tomorrow,
because of yesterday!
Open up the curtains, to
a fresh, and beautiful
new beginning.

Open Up

Open up to joy!
Open up to peace
Open up to the
beauty of the
season;
Open up to the,
wonders of nature!
Open up to love.

Ornamental Glow

A floral sparkle,
of ornamental
beauty!
A rosey starry
glow!
Sweet-n-Satiny!
In joyful
wonders!
He makes all
things,
beautiful.

Out In The Garden

Out in the garden, merry and bright!
Out in the garden, feeding the bees,
Out in the garden, radiating joy!
Out in the garden, kissed by the sun!
Out in the garden, for a season!
It's what we do, as flowers, out in,
the garden.

Our Purpose

We are created to,
Bring Beauty, Bring Joy!
Created to love!
Created to add fancy and zest!
Created to add colour and fun,
wherever we grow;
Created to give hope!
Created in love!

Pearls In Bloom

Sweet glazy blooms!
Pearls of the garden!
Sapphire and Spinels,
in fanciful blooms,
Sweet floral scents,
Reaching out in love!
Let the songs of love,
be heard!
For beauty is a,
definition of love.

Pearly And Precious

Pearly and Precious!
Regal in bloom,
It's a Summer's song!
It's a love gift,
It's a garden glow!
Pearly and Precious!
In love's garden she
stands!

Petally Regally

"Frilly, Flamboyant, and Elegant!"
Spreading out in floral grandeur,
A glorious flower of dawn!
Filled with energizing notes!
A colourful touch of joy.

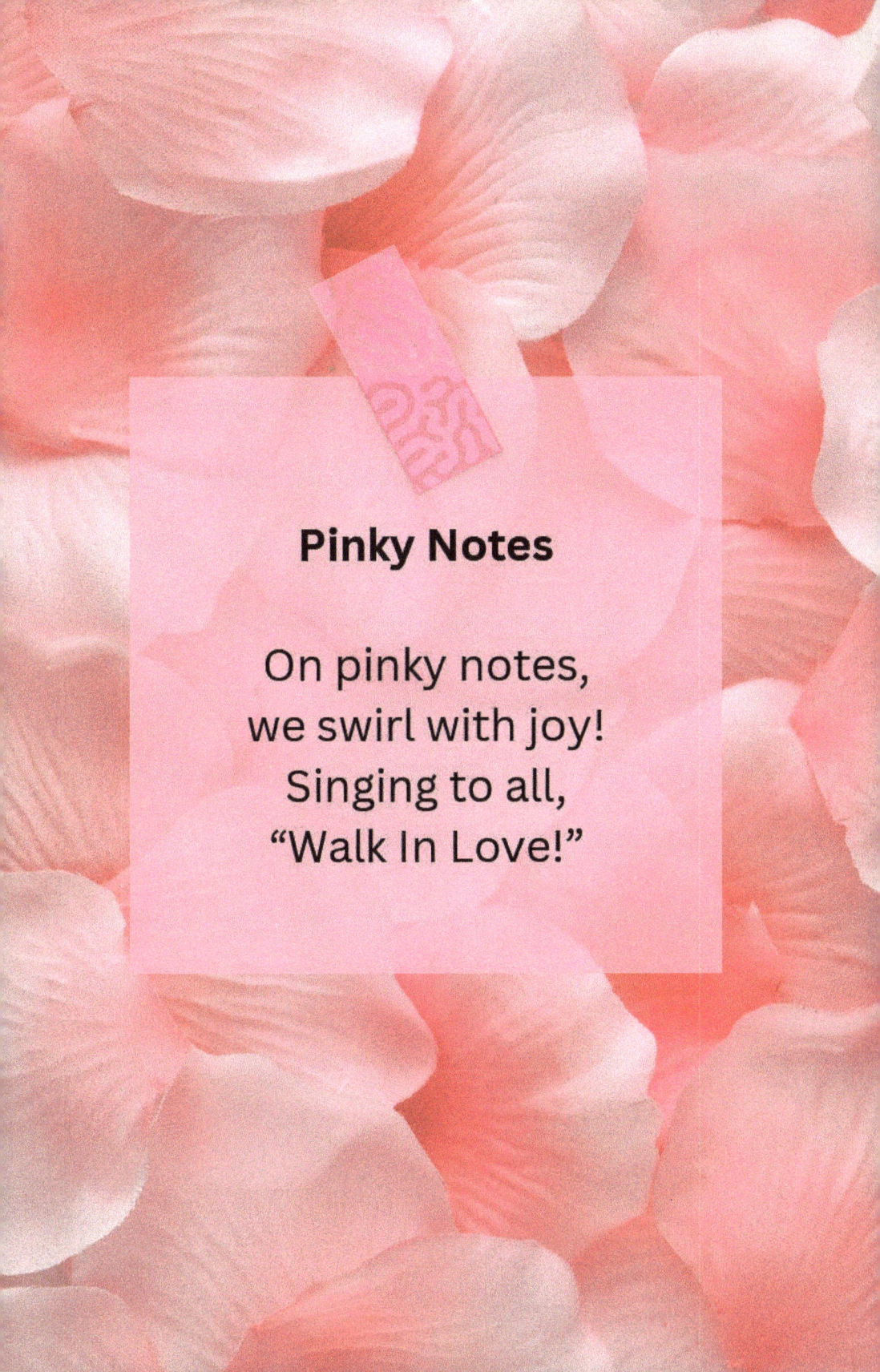

Pinky Notes

On pinky notes,
we swirl with joy!
Singing to all,
"Walk In Love!"

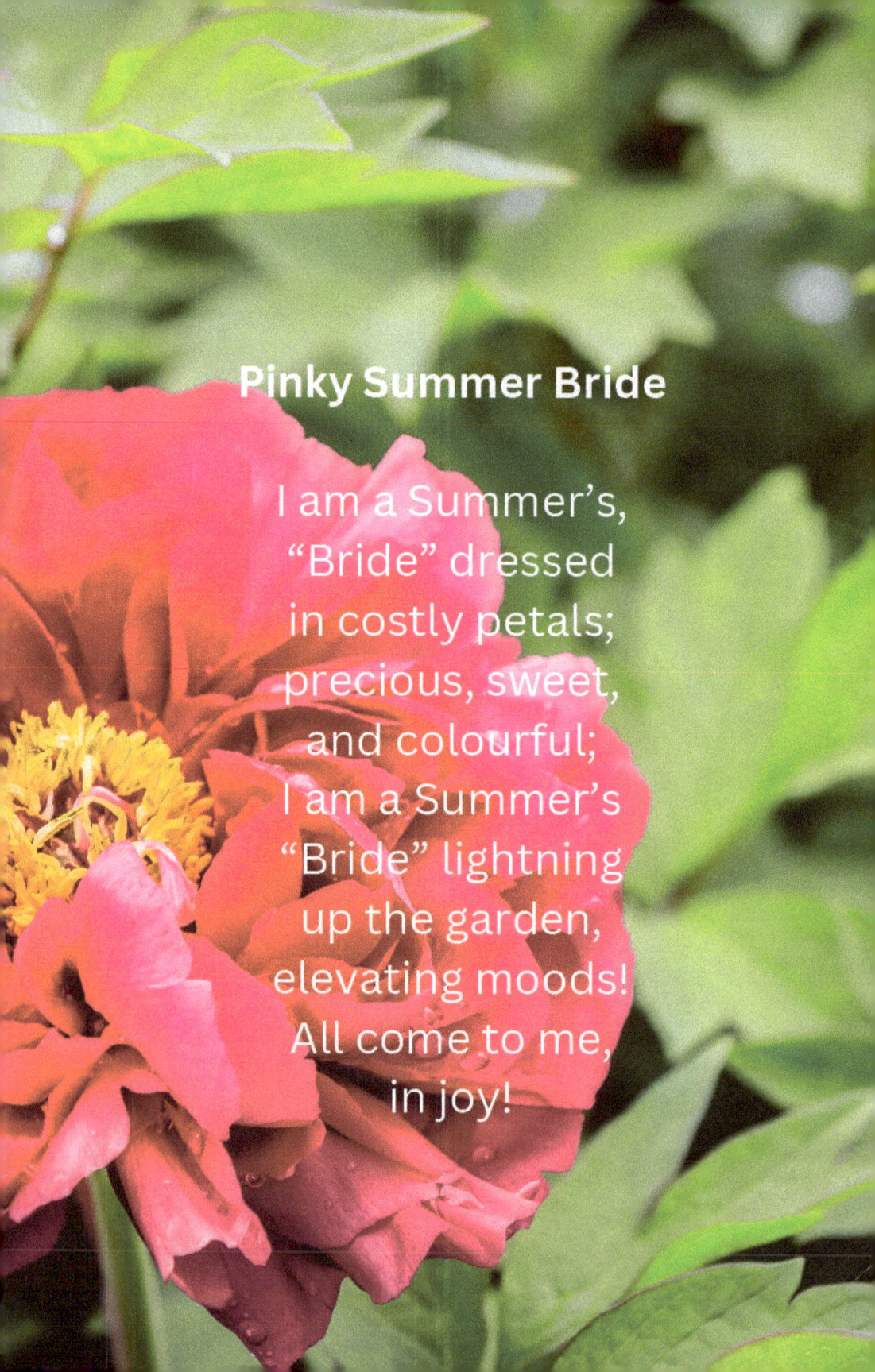

Pinky Summer Bride

I am a Summer's,
"Bride" dressed
in costly petals;
precious, sweet,
and colourful;
I am a Summer's
"Bride" lightning
up the garden,
elevating moods!
All come to me,
in joy!

Precious Book

Life is a golden book,
let's make its pages memorable!
Life is a beautiful book,
let's paint its pages gracefully...
Let's live its pages...
on golden notes of joy!
in sweet scents of love!
Life is a precious book,
let's handle it with care.

Precious Elites

Precious elites
of the garden!
Pink and White,
Opals in glow!
Sweet blooms,
of Summer,
Precious for
all to see.

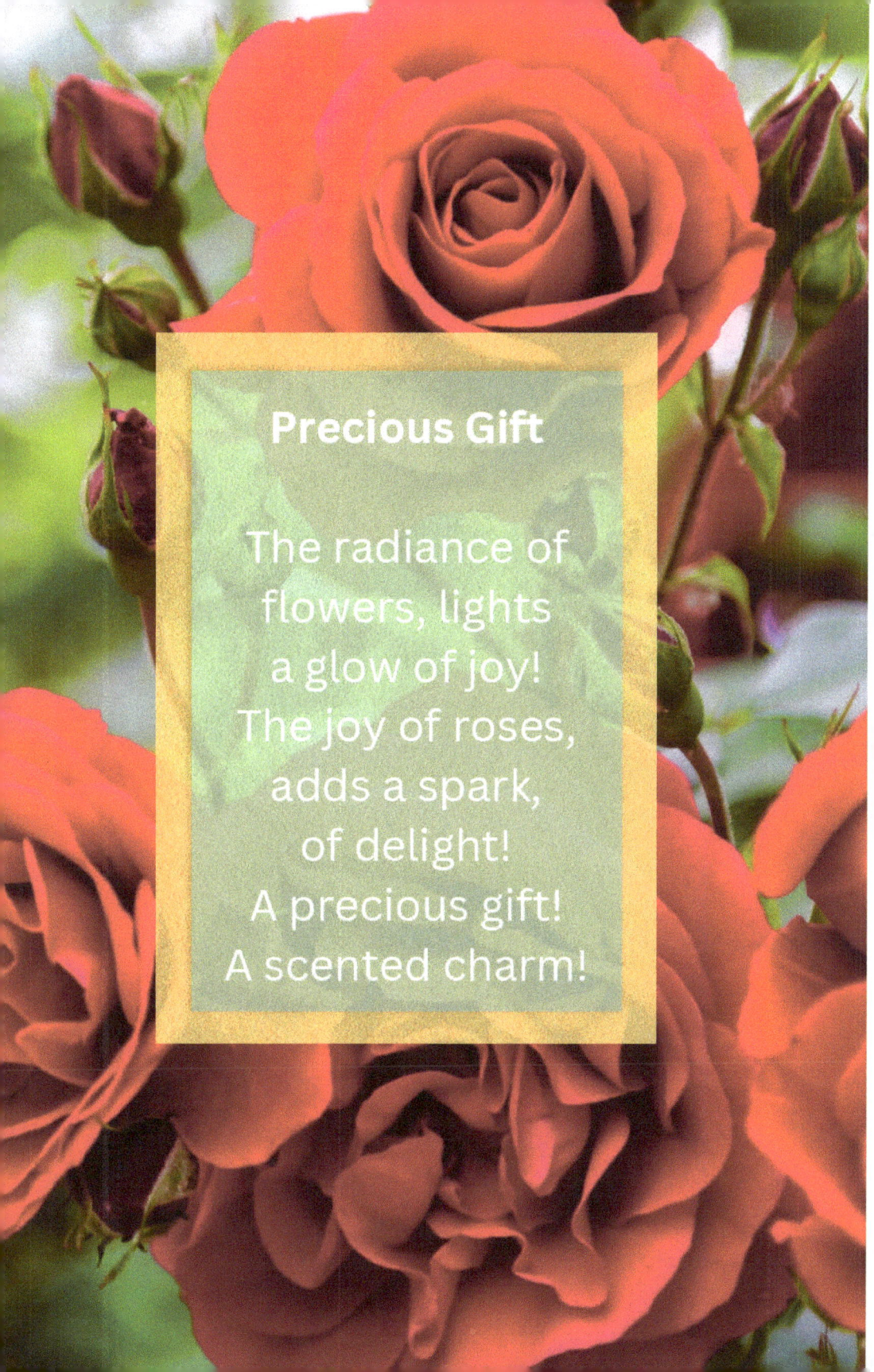

Precious Gift

The radiance of
flowers, lights
a glow of joy!
The joy of roses,
adds a spark,
of delight!
A precious gift!
A scented charm!

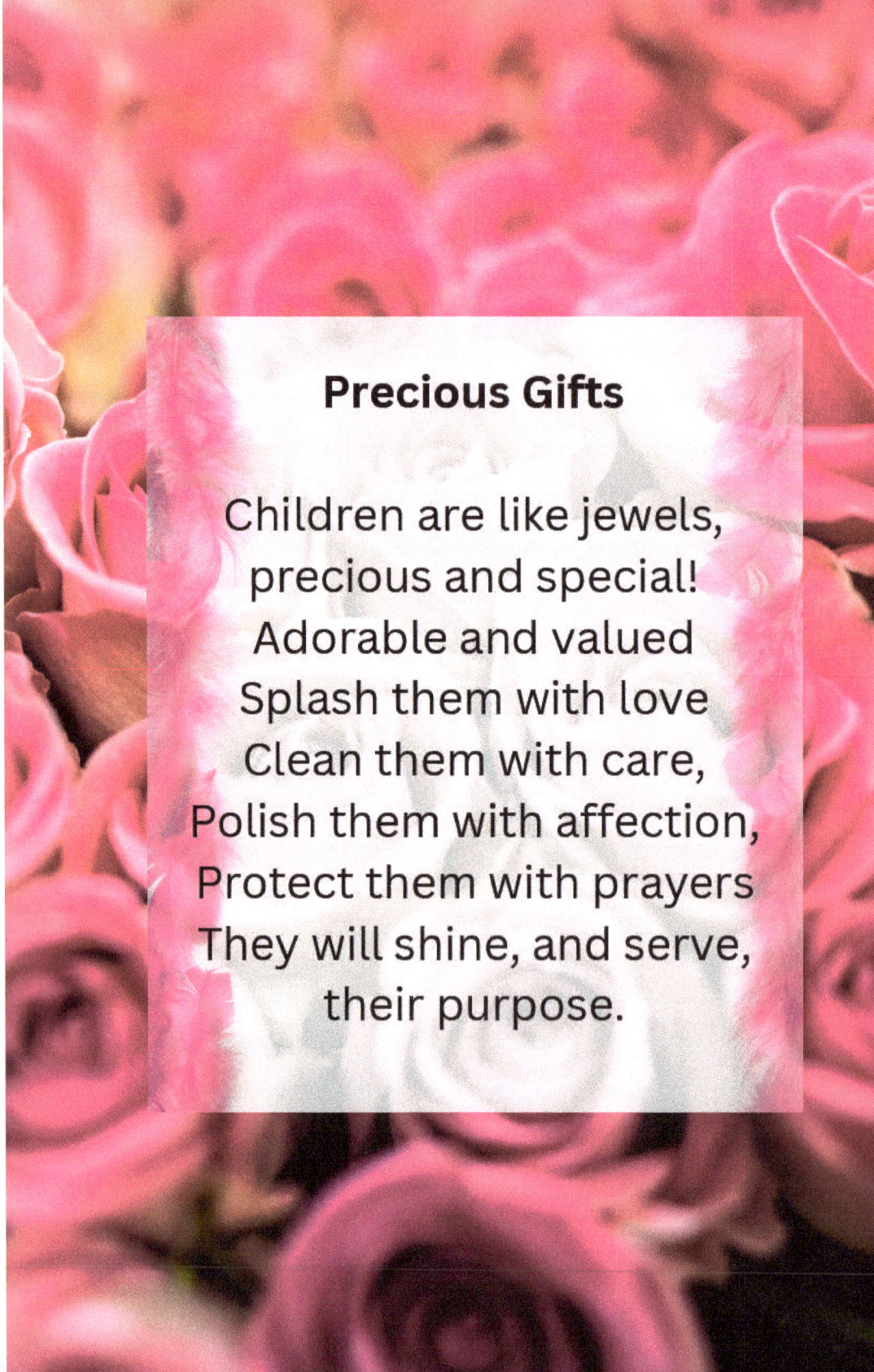

Precious Gifts

Children are like jewels,
precious and special!
Adorable and valued
Splash them with love
Clean them with care,
Polish them with affection,
Protect them with prayers
They will shine, and serve,
their purpose.

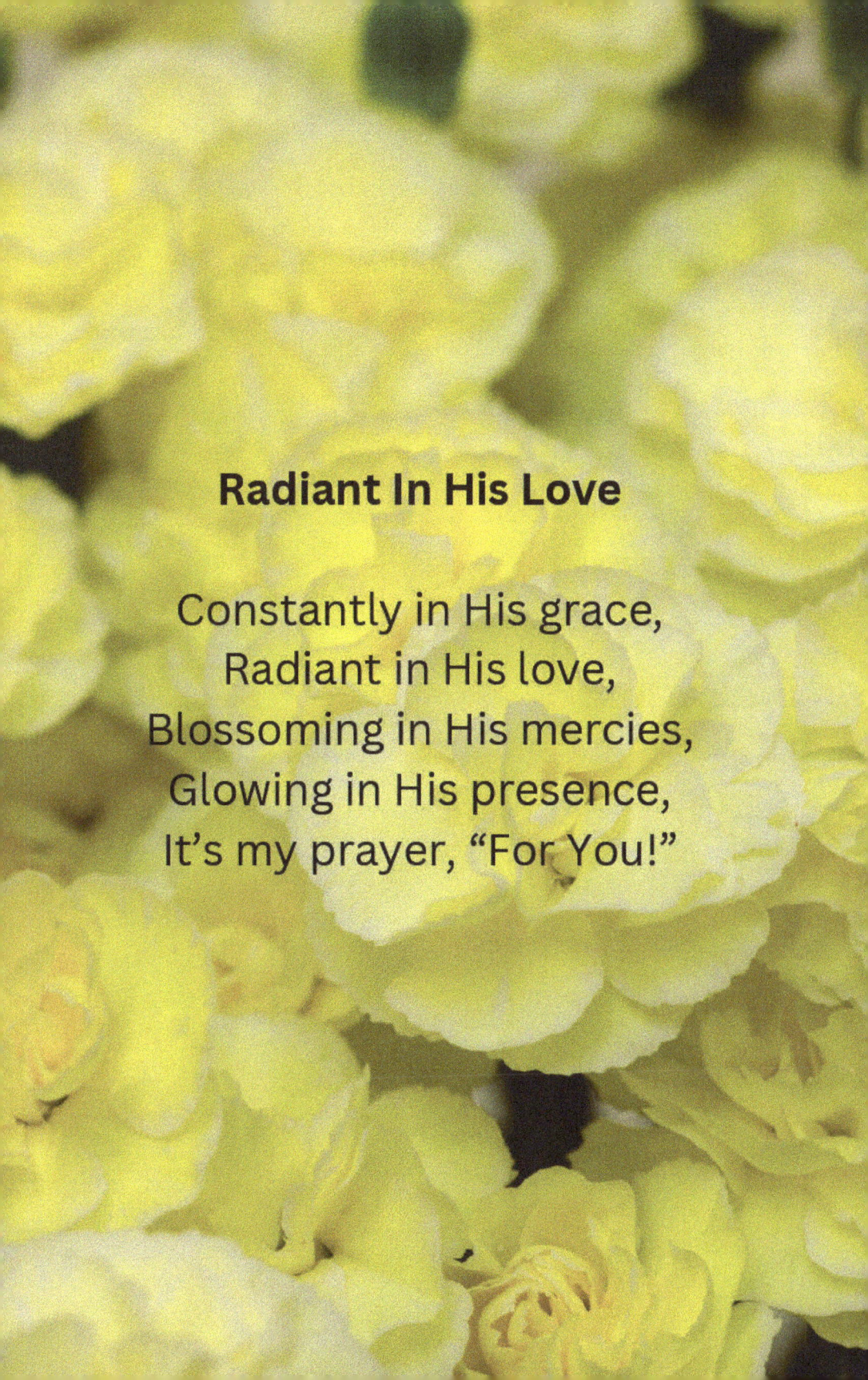

Radiant In His Love

Constantly in His grace,
Radiant in His love,
Blossoming in His mercies,
Glowing in His presence,
It's my prayer, "For You!"

Radiant Joy

In the abundance of His mercies,
we flourish beautifully!
In the glow of His grace,
we bloom radiantly!
In the radiance of His love,
we glorify His name!

Rainbow In The Sky

There is a rainbow, in the sky!
There is a song of hope, in the
heavens!
There is a rainbow in the sky!
God's favor, is being renewed.

Rhythms Of Joy

Sing on,
The wonders,
of His love!
Sing love,
loudly:
Sing love,
boldly.

Rosa Bells

Sweet "Rosa Bells,"
Dainties of the garden!
Touching hearts in joy,
Touching moments,
in beauty!
Rosa crystals in glow,
A wonder of the,
moment!
Joy of the season.

Rose Touch

Sing a rosey song,
Sing a love tune!
Sing a sweet note!
When the roses,
come out to play.

Rosey Date

Sing me a song!
Sing me a song
of joy!
Sing me a song
on Saturday,
When the roses,
dress for a date!

Rosey Glow

Rose Quartz in bloomy splendor,
In juicy glow they attract bees!
In warming glow they win hearts!
In gentle glow they light joy!
Pink crystals in rosey glow.

Ruby In Love

Love lies in
the heart of
flowers, with
a sweet glow!

Scent Of Florals

May your pathway,
be lit with the
scent of floral notes!
In the refreshing of
His love, may you
find joy.

Scent Of Ornaments

Jewels in the garden, radiant in
bloom!
Gemstones within reach,
Rubies and Emeralds flourishing
in bloom;
Blossoms exuding fragrances
that evokes joy!
Truly, flowers are the ornaments,
of the fields.

Shielded In Love

Keep me shielded
by your love,
O Lord,
Dip me in the
colours of
your love.

Sign In

Sign-in peace,
on a new day!
Sign-in love,
on a bloomy day!
Sign-in joy,
on a love sung day!
Sign-in hope,
on a merry rosey
day!

Signing In

Signing in as,
flowers;
We are made to love,
and to give joy!

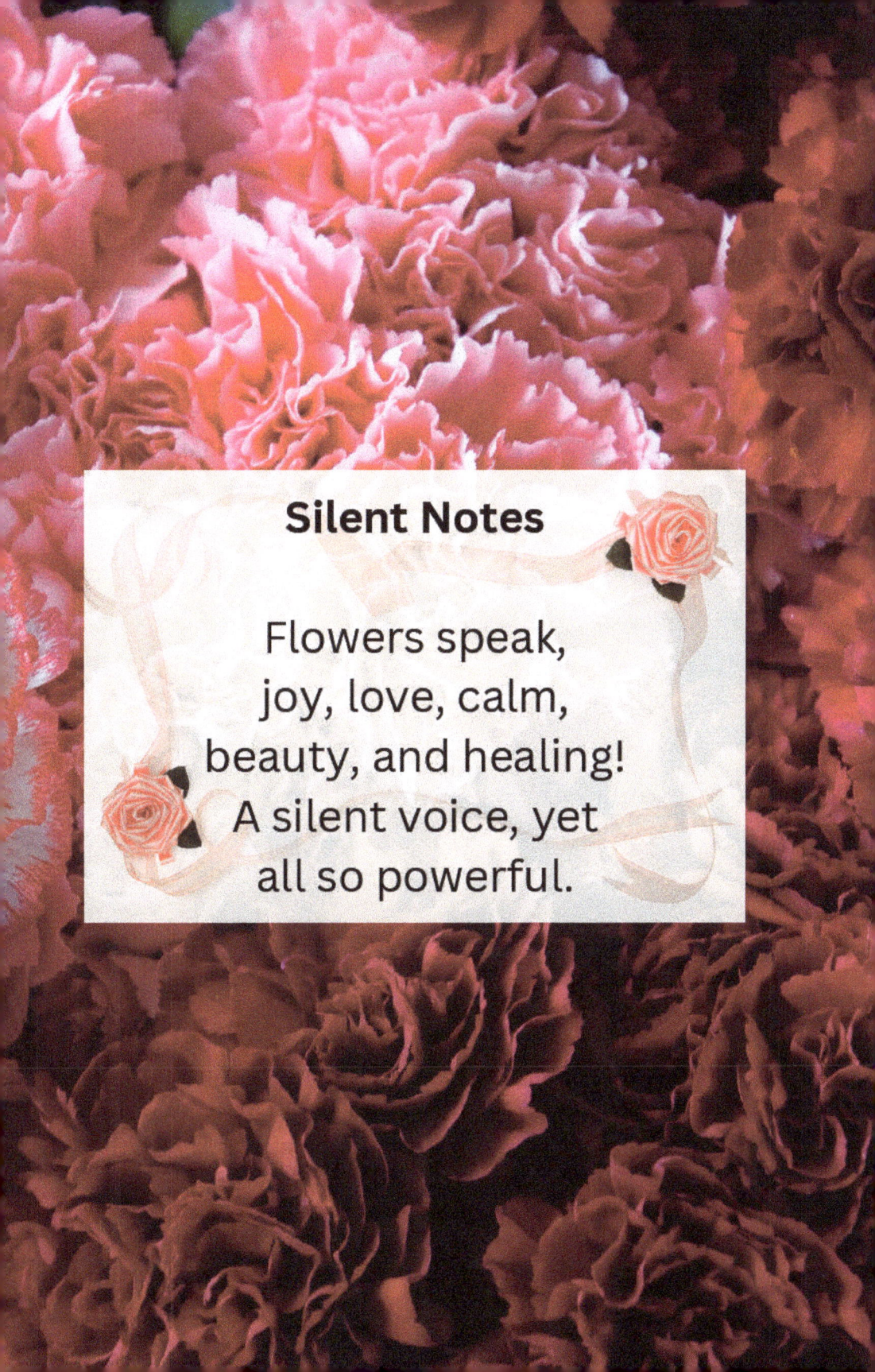

Silent Notes

Flowers speak,
joy, love, calm,
beauty, and healing!
A silent voice, yet
all so powerful.

Silent Whispers

Adorn me, with your beauty!
Cover me, with your love!
Divine is your fragrance,
Enchanting is the garden,
you grow;
For where beauty grows,
love is felt!

Singing Gems

Roses at dawn
Joy in bloom,
Love in petals!
Sweet notes
of precious
gems are
heard singing.

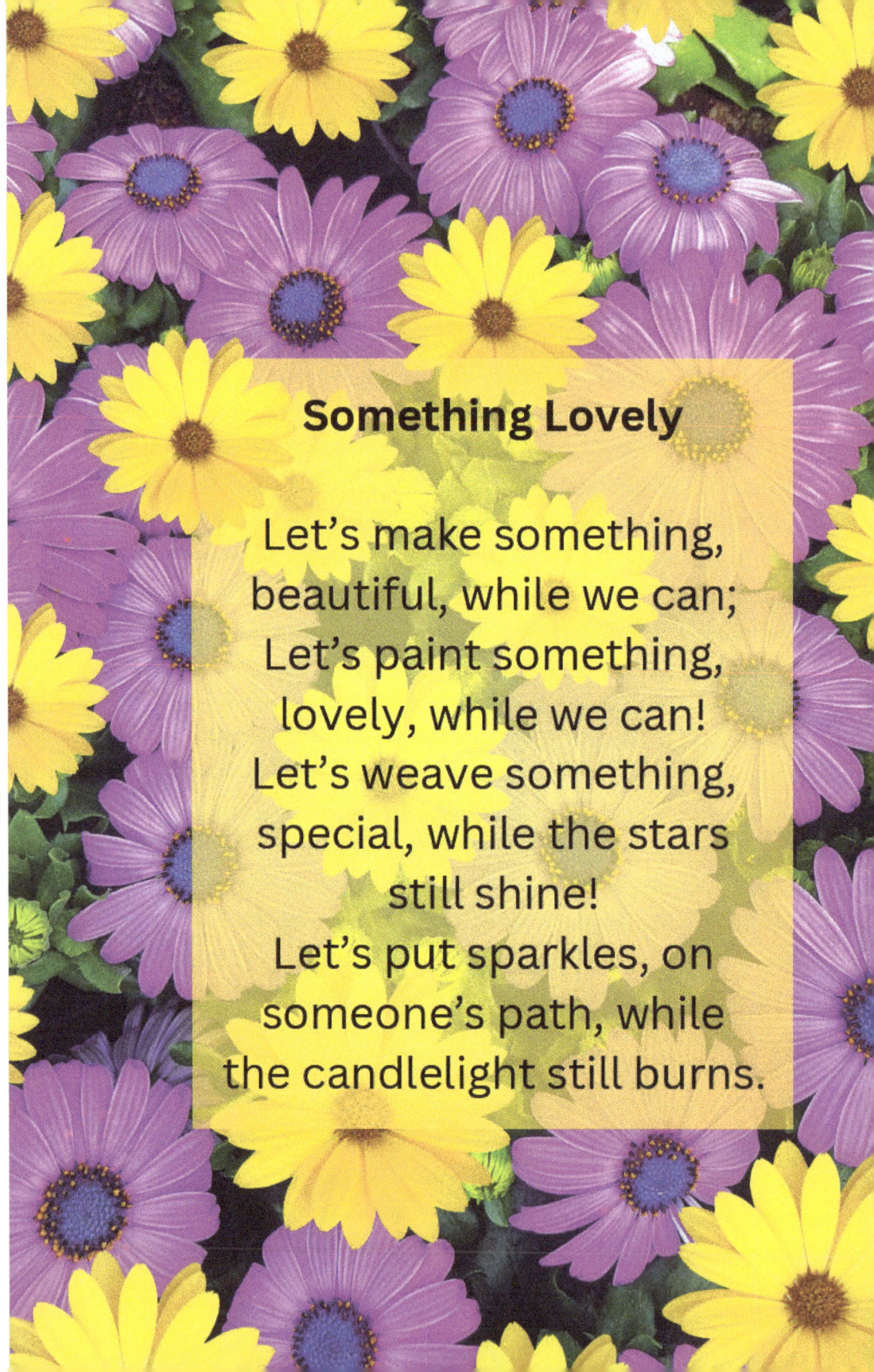

Something Lovely

Let's make something,
beautiful, while we can;
Let's paint something,
lovely, while we can!
Let's weave something,
special, while the stars
still shine!
Let's put sparkles, on
someone's path, while
the candlelight still burns.

Something Regal

Something Beautiful,
Something Precious,
Something Peachy,
Something Sweet!
Be yours always.

Songs Of Petals

"Stay Positive,
and
Happy."
"Stay Positive,
and
Strong."
"Stay Positive,
and
Blooming."
That's a flower's song.

Spacious Grounds

May the Lord,
take you to
spacious
grounds,
with an
outpouring
of love.

Sparkles And Sprinkles

Sparkles and Sprinkles,
Frilly rosey and sweet!
Like jewels on a tree!
It's a sparkle of joy!
It's a sprinkle of love!
It's a frilly rosey dance.

Sparkles Of Love

Love is
expressed from,
the fragrance
of roses;
Joy is
felt from the
petals of its
Love.

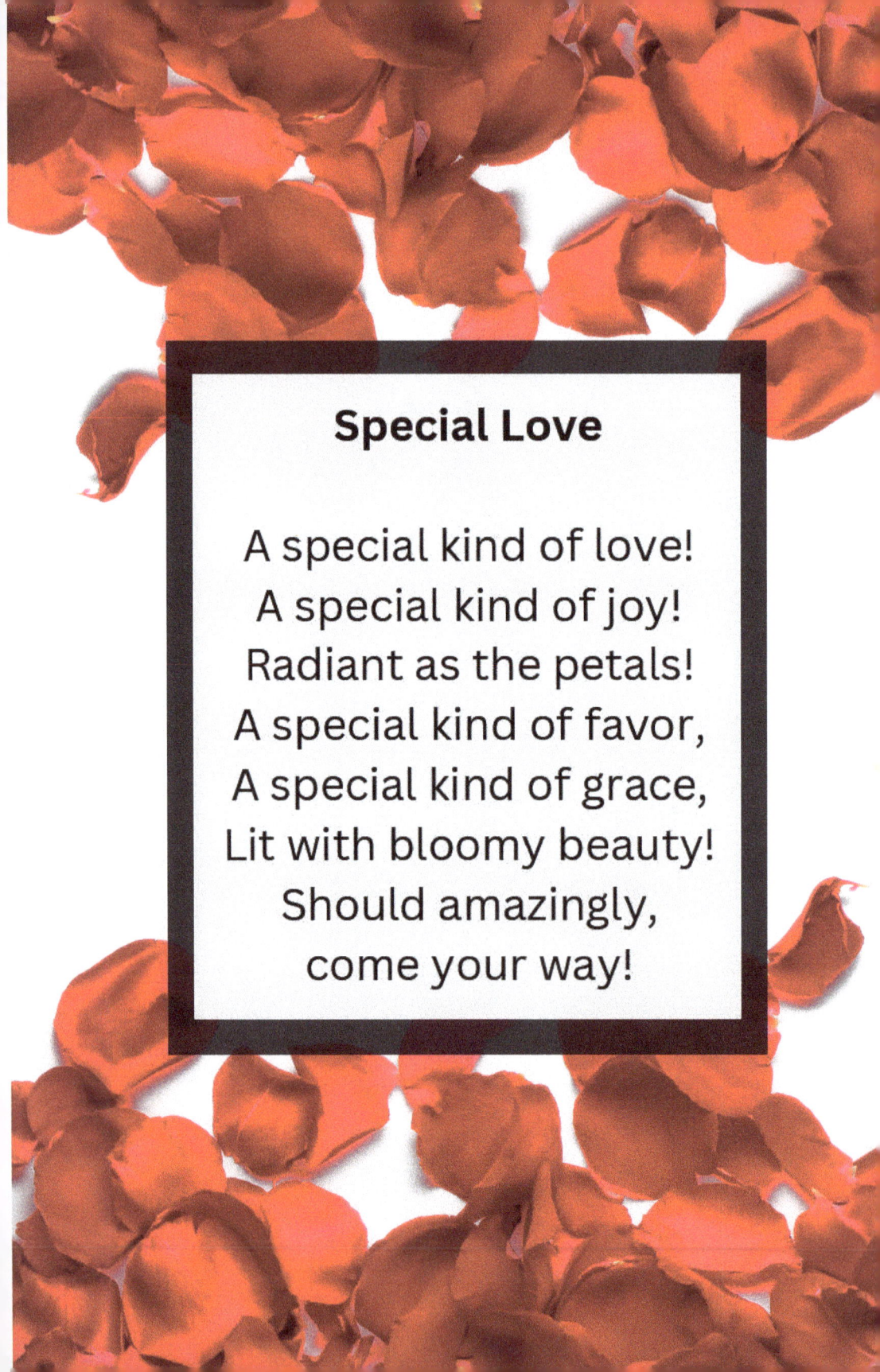

Special Love

A special kind of love!
A special kind of joy!
Radiant as the petals!
A special kind of favor,
A special kind of grace,
Lit with bloomy beauty!
Should amazingly,
come your way!

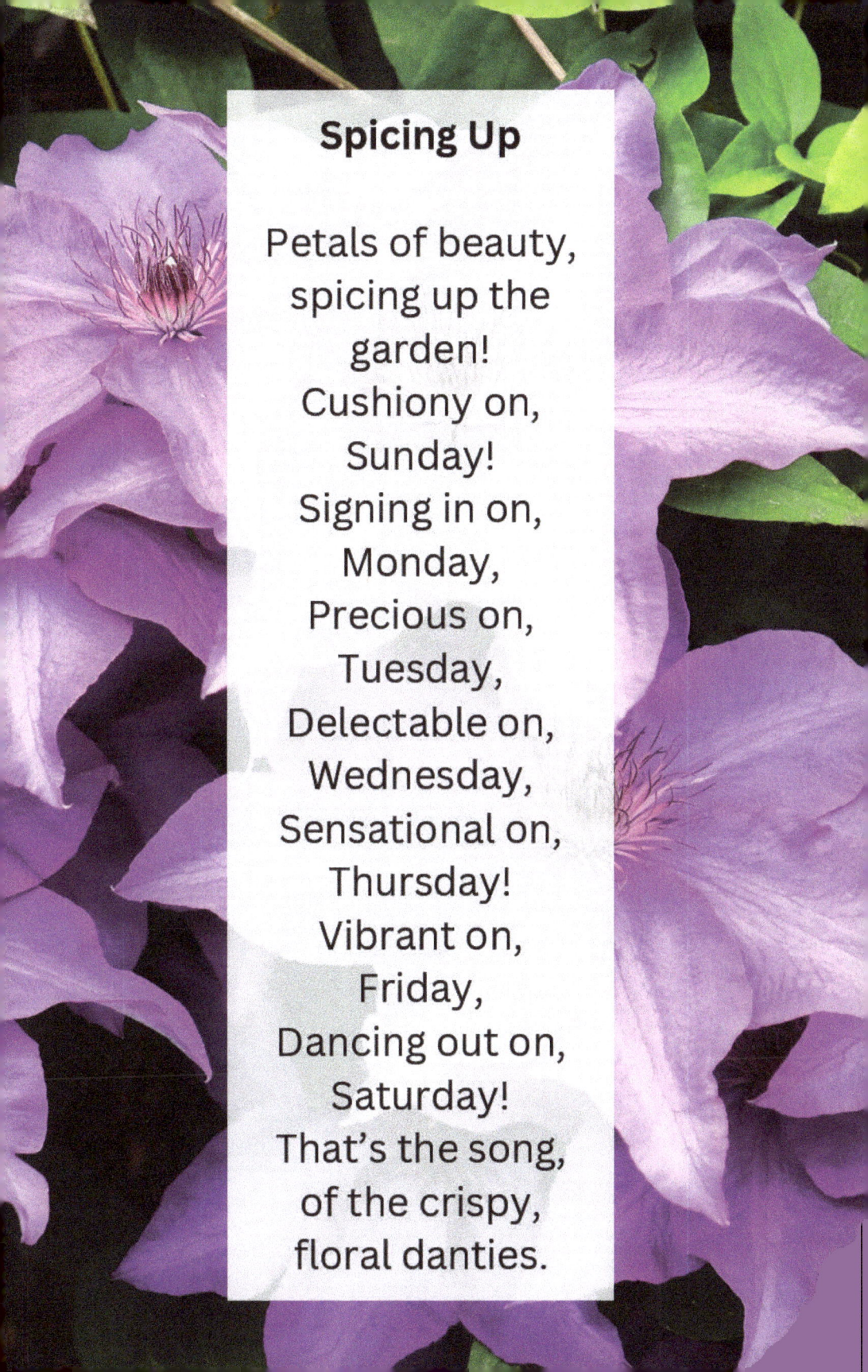

Spicing Up

Petals of beauty,
spicing up the
garden!
Cushiony on,
Sunday!
Signing in on,
Monday,
Precious on,
Tuesday,
Delectable on,
Wednesday,
Sensational on,
Thursday!
Vibrant on,
Friday,
Dancing out on,
Saturday!
That's the song,
of the crispy,
floral danties.

Splashs and Dips

I love the sound, of rain!
I love its splash, on my
petals!
It gives me, a blushing
pink!
It makes me grow in,
radiant colours;
I love the sound, of rain!
I thank Him, who sends,
down the rain.

Submerged In Love

May you be
submerged in the
the joy of His love.

Sweet Call

Seasons come,
twinkling in!
Sweet chimes,
in merry tunes!
A call to rise,
in roses!
A call to shine,
in blooms!
A call to glow,
in love!

Sweet Florals

It's the sound of
the rosey ride
i hear,
A swift click of
crispy petals!
Let the roses give
you a sweet ride
of floral essence!
A joyful ride of
love.

Sweet Flow

It's an oasis of grace,
Rhythms of joy!
Flowing as streams in
the valley!
Grace flows over us!
We are enveloped in
the aura of grace;
We are lit in love.

Sweet Glow

Sweetly,
and
Radiantly,
May
you glow!
in
His,
Love!

Sweet Love

In flourishing
beauty!
Sweetly as the
flowers,
May bountiful
blessings be
lit your way!

Sweet Ornaments

Sweet frilly lilies,
draped in white!
Joyous in bloom!
Wishing joy for all,
It's a time to
embrace love,
It's a time to
sing peace!
It's a time to
praise the
Lord, for all
He has done.

Sweet Return

It's a fluorescence of joy!
A fancy rosey glow,
A joyful treat for the bees!
The sweet return of roses,
A joyful touch of love.

Sweet Summer

Warm notes of roses on a sweet,
Summer ride; highlighting the
beauty of the season in joy!
Let it ring in love!

Sweet Touch

Sweet glaze of
cuddly blooms!
A reminiscence
of love!
An accolade to
bloomy beauty!
A joyful garden
wonder!
Touch me with
the scent of
your love.

Tale of Love

A flower is known by its name!
Each petal is a fabric of luxury!
Each bloom is a tale of love, an
evolution of hope!

Tender Love

Tenderly and adorably, she thrives in love.

Testament Of Love

Candied petally love notes!
Glazed by the glowing sun!
Laced with juicy berry tones,
Sparkly Rubies, in dancing
fields, of precious gems!
Corals in Rosey blooms!
A testament of love!

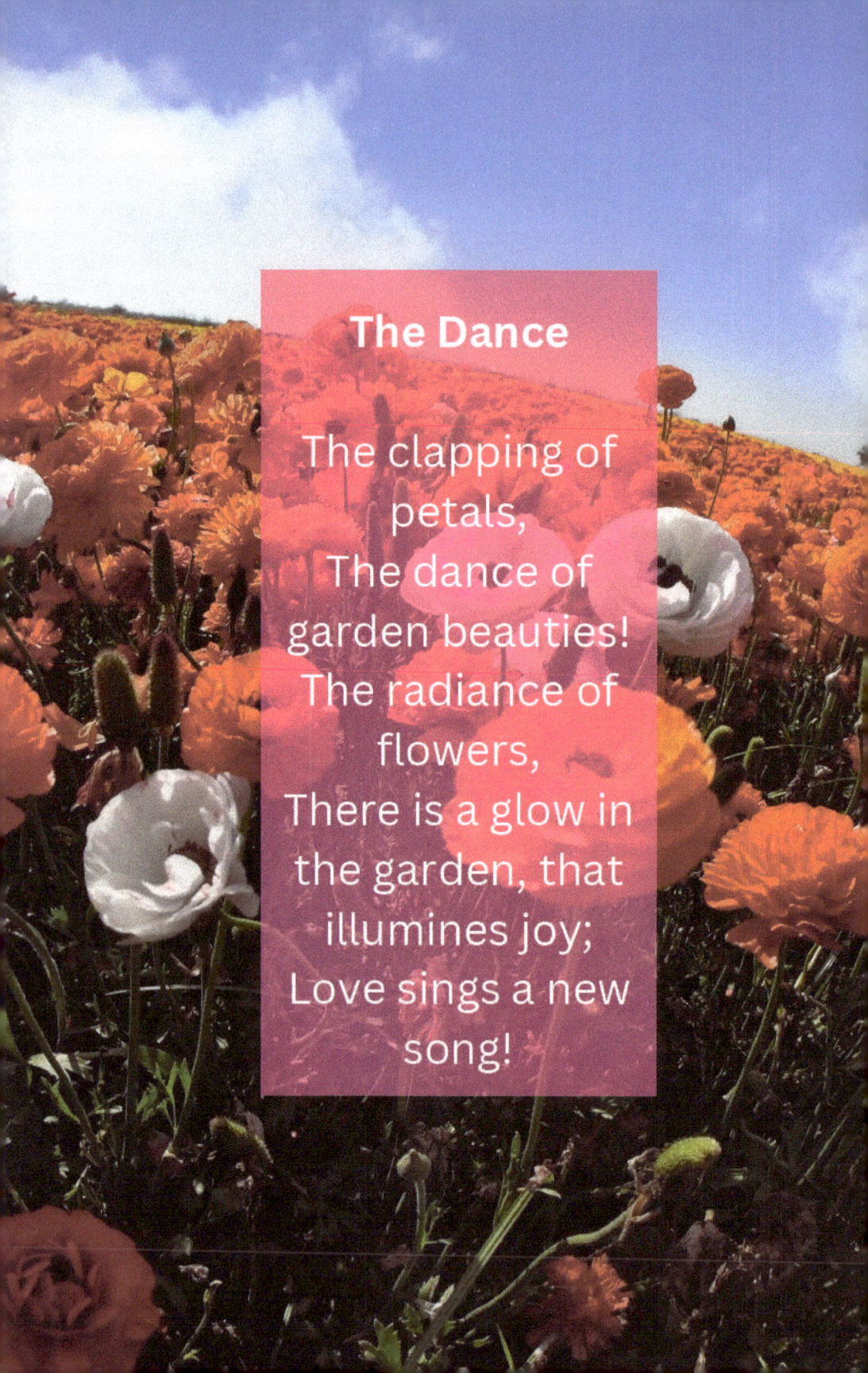

The Dance

The clapping of
petals,
The dance of
garden beauties!
The radiance of
flowers,
There is a glow in
the garden, that
illumines joy;
Love sings a new
song!

The Glowing Queen

Sweetly adorning the garden,
Graceful and radiant in white!
The "Glowing Queen!"
A stunning toast to Summer,
A whimsy glow of charm,
She radiates a joyful glow,
like a candlelight in the dark.
A glowy beauty treat!

Thousand Hills

Even the flowers on a thousand,
hills are His!
An artistic work, of the creator,
an awesome show, of His love!
Precious petals, filling the
heart, with warmth,
and joy!
Floral notes, enveloping
with an aura of love,
pleasure, and beauty;
A gift for all seasons!
A treasure for all times!

Toast To Love

Essence of floral
beauty!
An inspiration of
joy!
Charming and
adorable!
A toast to love!

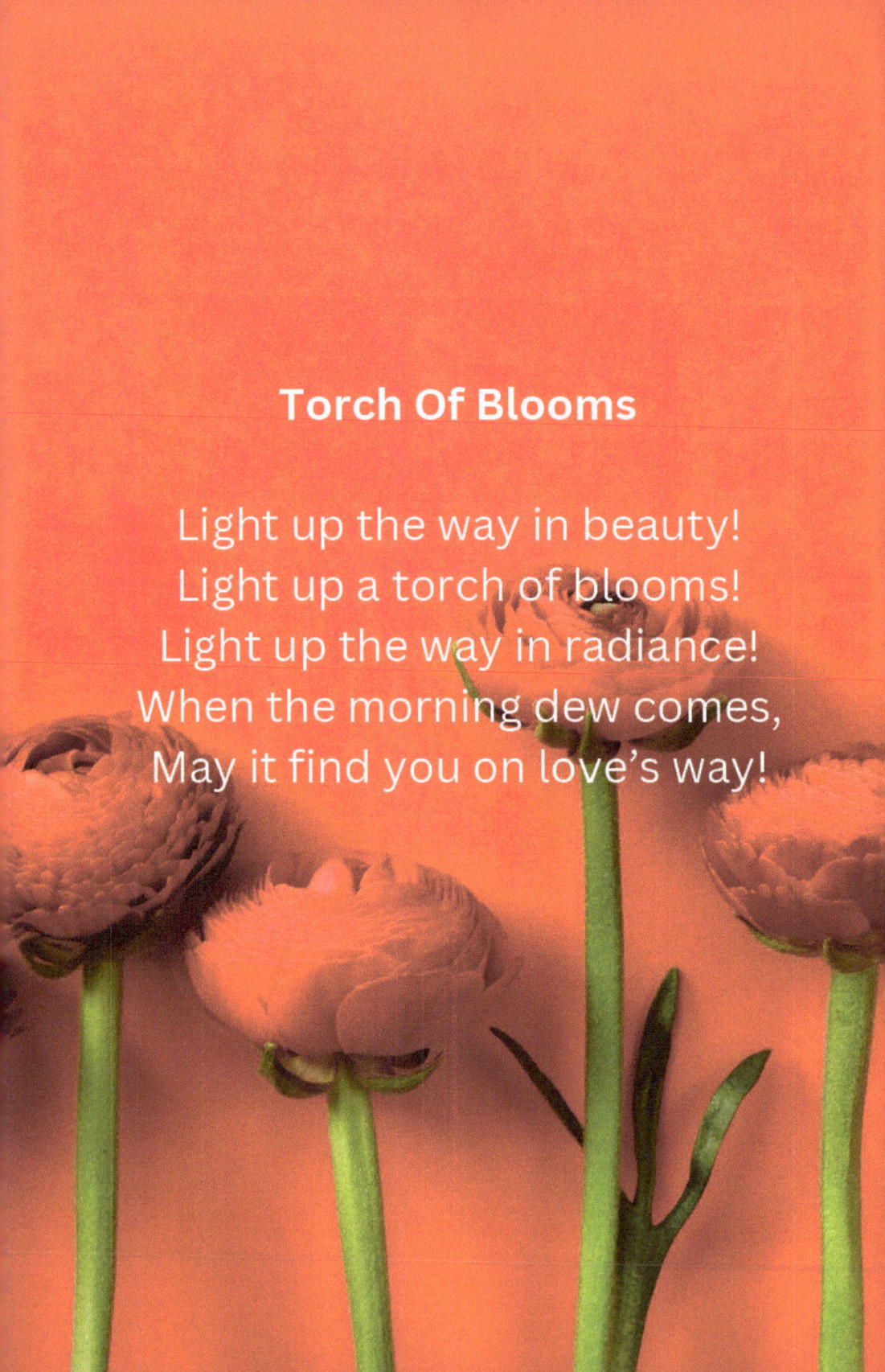

Torch Of Blooms

Light up the way in beauty!
Light up a torch of blooms!
Light up the way in radiance!
When the morning dew comes,
May it find you on love's way!

Touch Of Favor

The rain will come, as a touch
of blessing!
The dew will come, as a touch
of favor!
The glow will come, as a touch
of His love!
Joy will come, when radiance
shines through the skies!

Tunes Of Time

Flowers open at
a time!
Flourish at a time,
Fade at a time,
Time plays its
whispering,
notes for every
blooming beauty;
It's a breezy game,
of time!

Twinkles Of Love

Love comes twinkling,
on bloomy notes!
The colours of love plays
whimsical notes of cascading
tones of flowers...
In whispering floral accord melodious
tunes are heard, May the twinkly
bubbles of love come your way with
every touch of a bloomy gem.

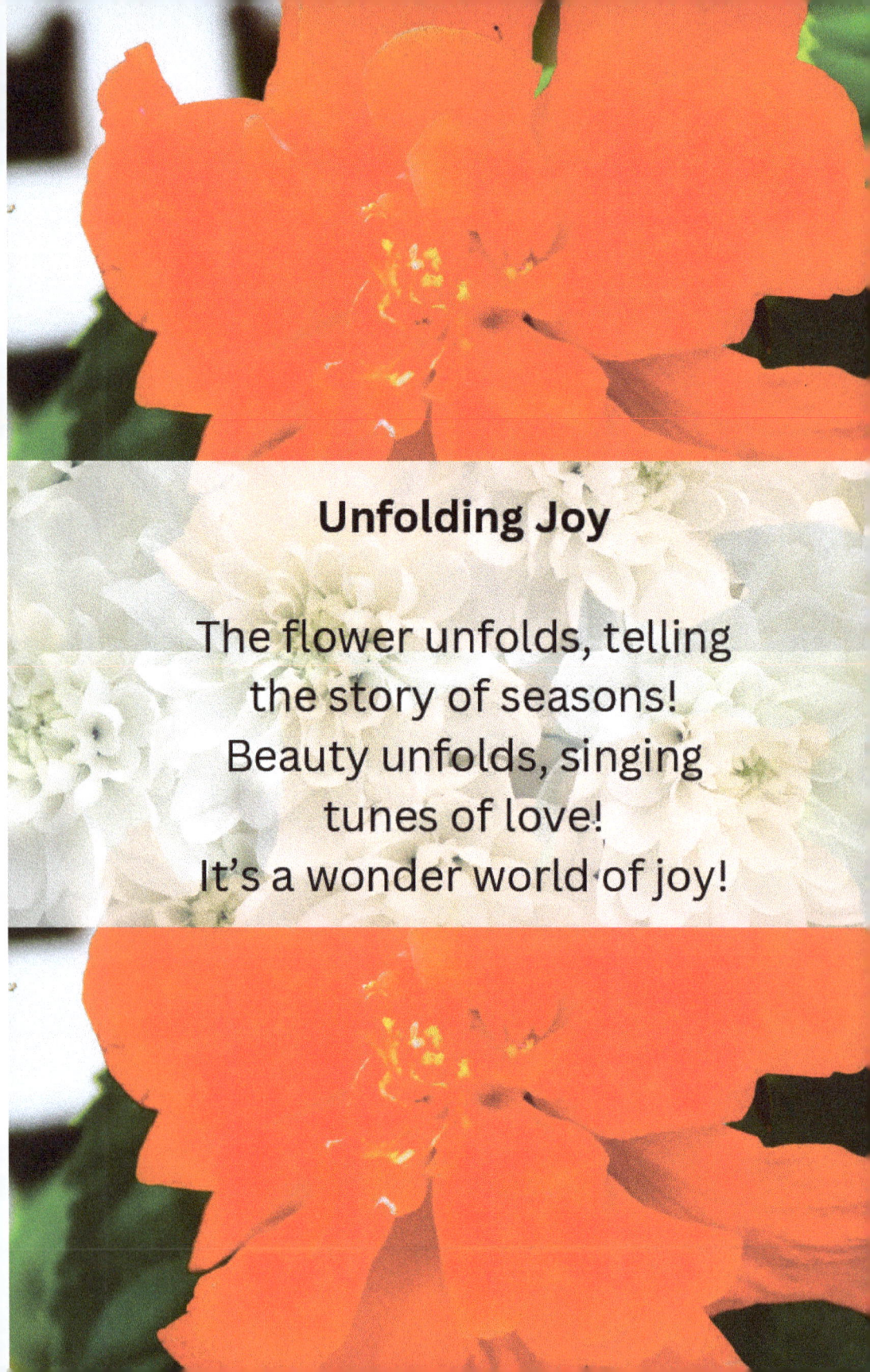

Unfolding Joy

The flower unfolds, telling
the story of seasons!
Beauty unfolds, singing
tunes of love!
It's a wonder world of joy!

Vibrant Love

Love writes it all on the tones of petals, It's the vibrancy of love, blooming bright when lit by the tones of many flowers.

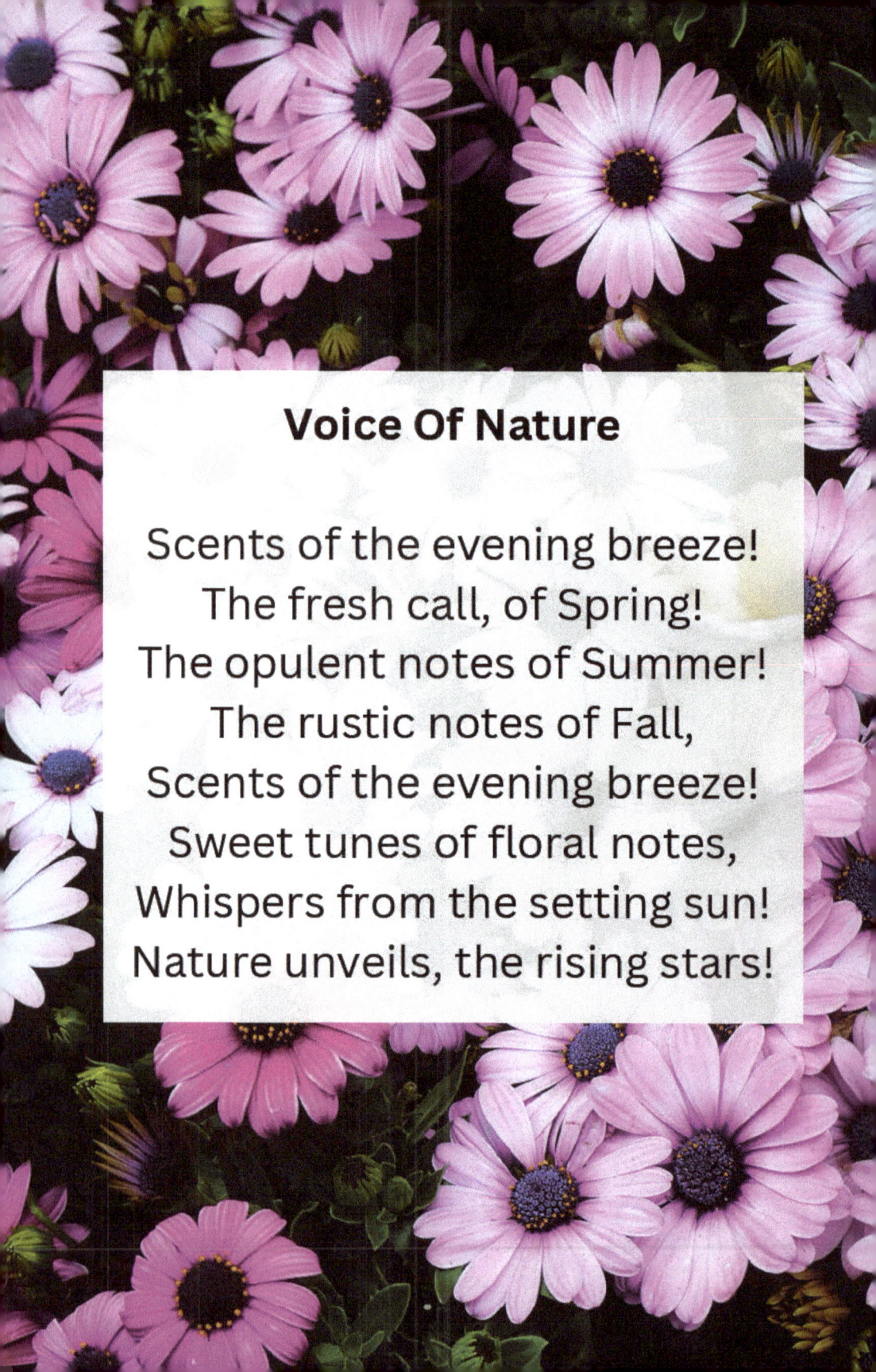

Voice Of Nature

Scents of the evening breeze!
The fresh call, of Spring!
The opulent notes of Summer!
The rustic notes of Fall,
Scents of the evening breeze!
Sweet tunes of floral notes,
Whispers from the setting sun!
Nature unveils, the rising stars!

Warm-n-Cheery

May the floral
flash of joy!
uplift you, with
warm-n-cheery,
notes.

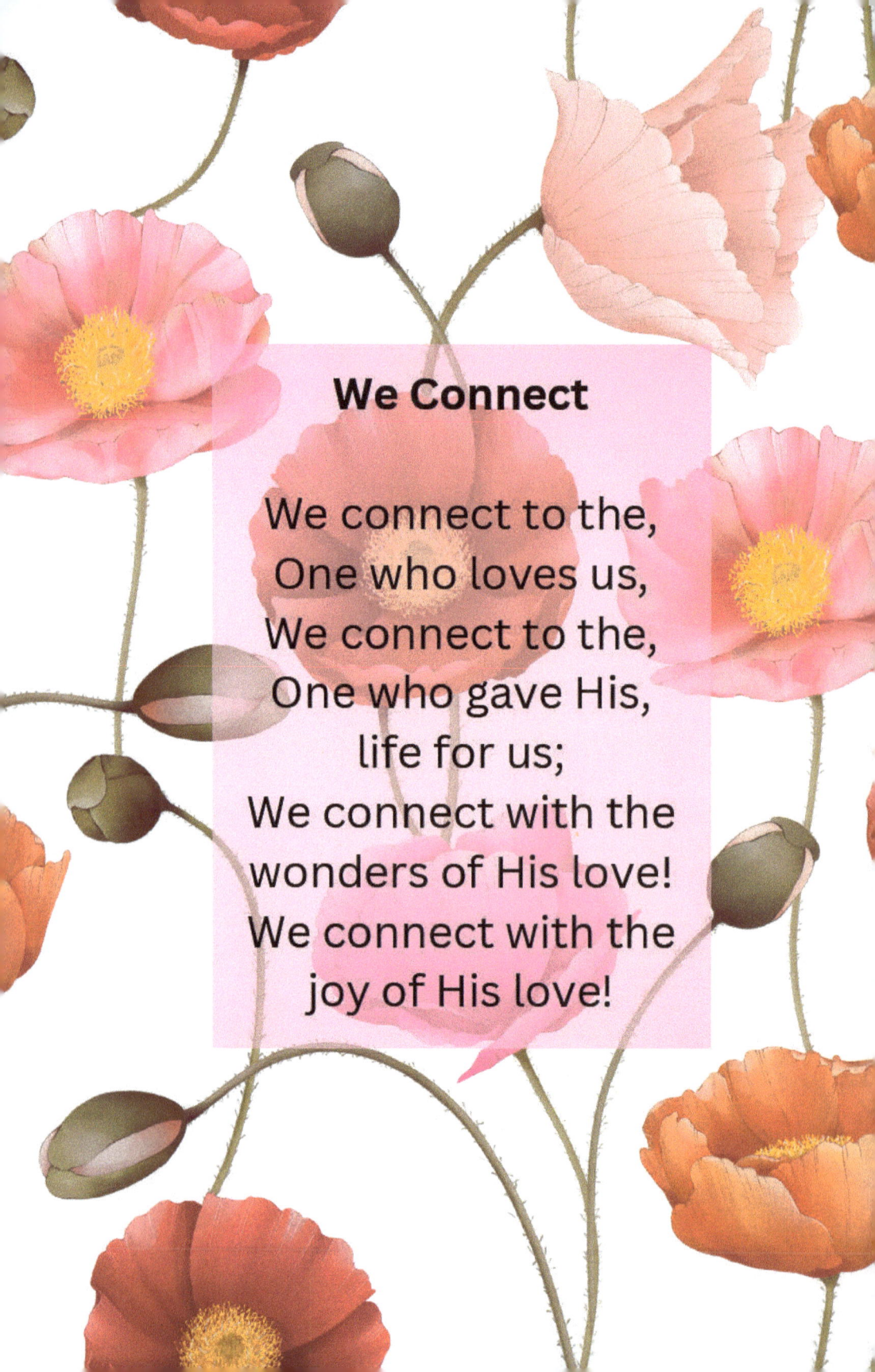

We Connect

We connect to the,
One who loves us,
We connect to the,
One who gave His,
life for us;
We connect with the
wonders of His love!
We connect with the
joy of His love!

Whimsical Garden

Plant in my garden, "Lilacs and Daisies,"
Plant in my garden, "Roses and Lilies,"
Plant in my garden, "Gingers and Tulips,"
Plant in my garden, "Carnations,"
Plant in my garden, "Honeysuckles,"
Plant in my garden, "Pansies,"
Plant in my garden, notes of
"Love and Joy"
"A Song."

With Thanks

With thanks we come!
In the warmth of the day,
we jubilate!
In the flourishing blooms, we find joy!
In love we come, to give
Him thanks, for all He
has done;
He provides for all,
He cares for all,
He loves all,
He sees all,
In joy we come, to give
Him thanks, for all;
He has done!

Wonder Garden

In the serenity of the garden,
I can feel His presence:
In the beauty of the garden,
I can feel His love!
Where the flowers grow!
Is a place I love to be.

Voice Of Corals

Beautiful are the corals that sing at dawn!
Voices echoing notes of florals, sweet, and soft!
Lovely are the precious petals, that beautify the garden, greeting yet another day.

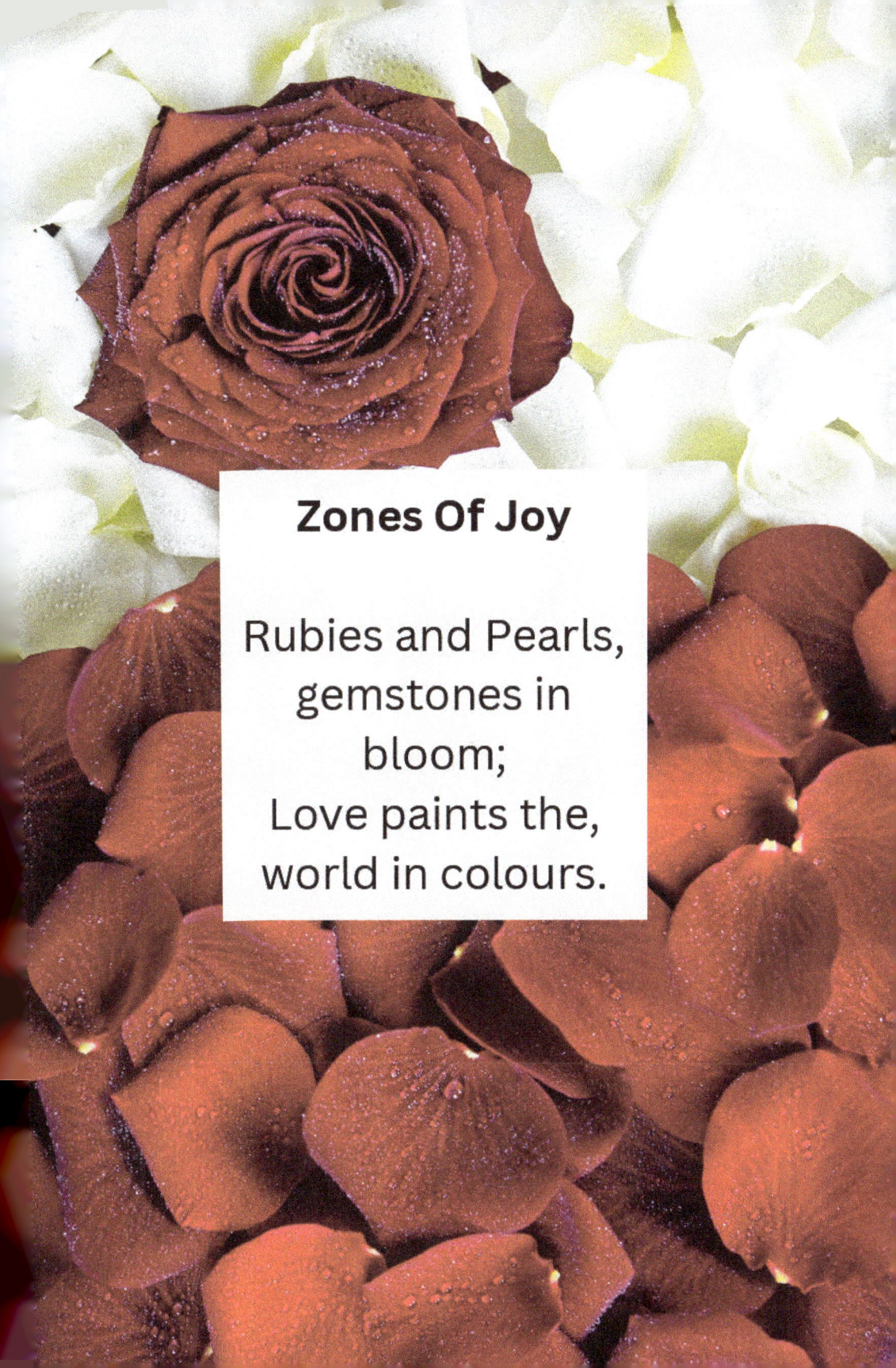

Zones Of Joy

Rubies and Pearls,
gemstones in
bloom;
Love paints the,
world in colours.

www.ingramcontent.com/pod-product-compliance
Lightning Source LLC
Chambersburg PA
CBHW041626140626
46547CB00030B/1054